P9-ECV-385

Mosaic 1

PARAGRAPH REVIEW AND
ESSAY DEVELOPMENT WRITING

Meredith Pike-Baky
Laurie Blass

Lawrence J. Zwier
Contributor, Focus on Testing

Meredith Pike-Baky
Writing Strand Leader

Mosaic 1 Writing, Silver Edition

ISBN 13: 978-0-07-353389-6 (Student Book)
ISBN 10: 0-07-353389-0
1 2 3 4 5 6 7 8 9 10 VNH 11 10 09 08 07 06

Editorial director: Erik Gundersen
Series editor: Valerie Kelemen
Developmental editor: Amy Lawler
Production manager: Juanita Thompson
Production coordinators: Vanessa Nuttry, James D. Gwyn
Cover designer: Robin Locke Monda
Interior designer: Nesbitt Graphics, Inc.
Photo researcher: Photoquick Research

The credits section for this book begins on page 220 and is considered an extension of the copyright page.

Cover photo: David Samuel Robbins/Corbis

A Special Thank You

The Interactions/Mosaic Silver Edition team wishes to thank our extended team: teachers, students, administrators, and teacher trainers, all of whom contributed invaluably to the making of this edition.

Macarena Aguilar, **North Harris College**, Houston, Texas ∎ Mohamad Al-Alam, **Imam Mohammad University**, Riyadh, Saudi Arabia ∎ Faisal M. Al Mohanna Abaalkhail, **King Saud University**, Riyadh, Saudi Arabia; Amal Al-Toaimy, **Women's College, Prince Sultan University**, Riyadh, Saudi Arabia ∎ Douglas Arroliga, **Ave Maria University**, Managua, Nicaragua ∎ Fairlie Atkinson, **Sungkyunkwan University**, Seoul, Korea ∎ Jose R. Bahamonde, **Miami-Dade Community College**, Miami, Florida ∎ John Ball, **Universidad de las Americas**, Mexico City, Mexico ∎ Steven Bell, **Universidad la Salle**, Mexico City, Mexico ∎ Damian Benstead, **Sungkyunkwan University**, Seoul, Korea ∎ Paul Cameron, **National Chengchi University**, Taipei, Taiwan R.O.C. ∎ Sun Chang, **Soongsil University**, Seoul, Korea ∎ Grace Chao, **Soochow University**, Taipei, Taiwan R.O.C. ∎ Chien Ping Chen, **Hua Fan University**, Taipei, Taiwan R.O.C. ∎ Selma Chen, **Chihlee Institute of Technology**, Taipei, Taiwan R.O.C. ∎ Sylvia Chiu, **Soochow University**, Taipei, Taiwan R.O.C. ∎ Mary Colonna, **Columbia University**, New York, New York ∎ Lee Culver, **Miami-Dade Community College,** Miami, Florida ∎ Joy Durighello, **City College of San Francisco**, San Francisco, California ∎ Isabel Del Valle, **ULATINA**, San Jose, Costa Rica ∎ Linda Emerson, **Sogang University**, Seoul, Korea ∎ Esther Entin, **Miami-Dade Community College**, Miami, Florida ∎ Glenn Farrier, **Gakushuin Women's College**, Tokyo, Japan ∎ Su Wei Feng, Taipei, Taiwan R.O.C. ∎ Judith Garcia, **Miami-Dade Community College**, Miami, Florida ∎ Maxine Gillway, **United Arab Emirates University**, Al Ain, United Arab Emirates ∎ Colin Gullberg, **Soochow University**, Taipei, Taiwan R.O.C. ∎ Natasha Haugnes, **Academy of Art University**, San Francisco, California ∎ Barbara Hockman, **City College of San Francisco**, San Francisco, California ∎ Jinyoung Hong, **Sogang University**, Seoul, Korea ∎ Sherry Hsieh, **Christ's College**, Taipei, Taiwan R.O.C. ∎ Yu-shen Hsu, **Soochow University**, Taipei, Taiwan R.O.C. ∎ Cheung Kai-Chong, **Shih-Shin University**, Taipei, Taiwan R.O.C. ∎ Leslie Kanberg, **City College of San Francisco**, San Francisco, California ∎ Gregory Keech, **City College of San Francisco**, San Francisco, California ∎ Susan Kelly, **Sogang University**, Seoul, Korea ∎ Myoungsuk Kim, **Soongsil University**, Seoul, Korea ∎ Youngsuk Kim, **Soongsil University**, Seoul, Korea ∎ Roy Langdon, **Sungkyunkwan University**, Seoul, Korea ∎ Rocio Lara, **University of Costa Rica**, San Jose, Costa Rica ∎ Insung Lee, **Soongsil University**, Seoul, Korea ∎ Andy Leung, **National Tsing Hua University**, Taipei, Taiwan R.O.C. ∎ Elisa Li Chan, **University of Costa Rica**, San Jose, Costa Rica ∎ Elizabeth Lorenzo, **Universidad Internacional de las Americas**, San Jose, Costa Rica ∎ Cheryl Magnant, **Sungkyunkwan University**, Seoul, Korea ∎ Narciso Maldonado Iuit, **Escuela Tecnica Electricista**, Mexico City, Mexico ∎ Shaun Manning, **Hankuk University of Foreign Studies**, Seoul, Korea ∎ Yoshiko Matsubayashi, **Tokyo International University**, Saitama, Japan ∎ Scott Miles, **Sogang University**, Seoul, Korea ∎ William Mooney, **Chinese Culture University**, Taipei, Taiwan R.O.C. ∎ Jeff Moore, **Sungkyunkwan University**, Seoul, Korea ∎ Mavelin de Moreno, **Lehnsen Roosevelt School**, Guatemala City, Guatemala ∎ Ahmed Motala, **University of Sharjah**, Sharjah, United Arab Emirates ∎ Carlos Navarro, **University of Costa Rica**, San Jose, Costa Rica ∎ Dan Neal, **Chih Chien University**, Taipei, Taiwan R.O.C. ∎ Margarita Novo, **University of Costa Rica**, San Jose, Costa Rica ∎ Karen O'Neill, **San Jose State University**, San Jose, California ∎ Linda O'Roke, **City College of San Francisco**, San Francisco, California ∎ Martha Padilla, **Colegio de Bachilleres de Sinaloa,** Culiacan, Mexico ∎ Allen Quesada, **University of Costa Rica**, San Jose, Costa Rica ∎ Jim Rogge, **Broward Community College**, Ft. Lauderdale, Florida ∎ Marge Ryder, **City College of San Francisco**, San Francisco, California ∎ Gerardo Salas, **University of Costa Rica**, San Jose, Costa Rica ∎ Shigeo Sato, **Tamagawa University**, Tokyo, Japan ∎ Lynn Schneider, **City College of San Francisco**, San Francisco, California ∎ Devan Scoble, **Sungkyunkwan University**, Seoul, Korea ∎ Maryjane Scott, **Soongsil University**, Seoul, Korea ∎ Ghaida Shaban, **Makassed Philanthropic School**, Beirut, Lebanon ∎ Maha Shalok, **Makassed Philanthropic School**, Beirut, Lebanon ∎ John Shannon, **University of Sharjah**, Sharjah, United Arab Emirates ∎ Elsa Sheng, **National Technology College of Taipei**, Taipei, Taiwan R.O.C. ∎ Ye-Wei Sheng, **National Taipei College of Business**, Taipei, Taiwan R.O.C. ∎ Emilia Sobaja, **University of Costa Rica**, San Jose, Costa Rica ∎ You-Souk Yoon, **Sungkyunkwan University**, Seoul, Korea ∎ Shanda Stromfield, **San Jose State University**, San Jose, California ∎ Richard Swingle, **Kansai Gaidai College**, Osaka, Japan ∎ Carol Sung, **Christ's College**, Taipei, Taiwan R.O.C. ∎ Jeng-Yih Tim Hsu, **National Kaohsiung First University of Science and Technology**, Kaohsiung, Taiwan R.O.C. ∎ Shinichiro Torikai, **Rikkyo University**, Tokyo, Japan ∎ Sungsoon Wang, **Sogang University**, Seoul, Korea ∎ Kathleen Wolf, **City College of San Francisco**, San Francisco, California ∎ Sean Wray, **Waseda University International**, Tokyo, Japan ∎ Belinda Yanda, **Academy of Art University**, San Francisco, California ∎ Su Huei Yang, **National Taipei College of Business**, Taipei, Taiwan R.O.C. ∎ Tzu Yun Yu, **Chungyu Institute of Technology**, Taipei, Taiwan R.O.C.

Author Acknowledgements

Grateful acknowledgements to: Erik Gundersen, Valerie Kelemen,
Amy Lawler, Jennifer Wilson, Mari Vargo, and strand leaders Pam Hartmann
and Jami Hanreddy.

I would like to profusely thank Susan Johnson for her skillful editing
on the Mosaic 1 TE.

To Alex, Sarah, and Nick who grew up alongside Mosaic and have become more
helpful, more thoughtful, and more gratifying—just like the Silver Edition!

Table of Contents

v

Welcome to Interactions/Mosaic Silver Edition

Interactions/Mosaic **Silver Edition** is a fully-integrated, 18-book academic skills series. Language proficiencies are articulated from the beginning through advanced levels <u>within</u> each of the four language skill strands. Chapter themes articulate <u>across</u> the four skill strands to systematically recycle content, vocabulary, and grammar.

NEW to the Silver Edition:

- **World's most popular and comprehensive academic skills series—** thoroughly updated for today's global learners
- **New design** showcases compelling instructional photos to strengthen the educational experience
- **Enhanced focus on vocabulary building, test taking, and critical thinking skills** promotes academic achievement
- **New strategies and activities for the TOEFL®iBT** build invaluable test taking skills
- **New "Best Practices" approach** promotes excellence in language teaching

NEW to Mosaic 1 Writing:

- **All new content:**—Chapter 2 Cooperation and Competition
- **Transparent chapter structure** with consistent part headings, activity labeling, and clear guidance—strengthens the academic experience:

  Part 1: Preparing to Write
  Part 2: Focusing on Words and Phrases
  Part 3: Organizing and Developing Your Ideas
  Part 4: Evaluating Your Writing

- **Writing Articulation Chart** (inside back cover) shows how the four Writing books lead students from successful sentence building to effective academic essay writing
- **Systematically structured, multi-step *Writing Process*** culminates in a *Writing Product* task
- **New communicative activities** invite students to interact meaningfully with target words to build vocabulary skills for writing
- **New self-evaluation rubric** for each chapter supports the learner as he or she builds confidence and autonomy in academic writing

---

* TOEFL is a registered trademark of Educational Testing Service (ETS). This publication is not endorsed or approved by ETS.

Interactions/Mosaic
Best Practices

Our Interactions/Mosaic Silver Edition team has produced an edition that focuses on Best Practices, principles that contribute to excellent language teaching and learning. Our team of writers, editors, and teacher consultants has identified the following six interconnected Best Practices:

Making Use of Academic Content

Materials and tasks based on academic content and experiences give learning real purpose. Students explore real world issues, discuss academic topics, and study content-based and thematic materials.

Organizing Information

Students learn to organize thoughts and notes through a variety of graphic organizers that accommodate diverse learning and thinking styles.

Scaffolding Instruction

A scaffold is a physical structure that facilitates construction of a building. Similarly, scaffolding instruction is a tool used to facilitate language learning in the form of predictable and flexible tasks. Some examples include oral or written modeling by the teacher or students, placing information in a larger framework, and reinterpretation.

Activating Prior Knowledge

Students can better understand new spoken or written material when they connect to the content. Activating prior knowledge allows students to tap into what they already know, building on this knowledge, and stirring a curiosity for more knowledge.

Interacting with Others

Activities that promote human interaction in pair work, small group work, and whole class activities present opportunities for real world contact and real world use of language.

Cultivating Critical Thinking

Strategies for critical thinking are taught explicitly. Students learn tools that promote critical thinking skills crucial to success in the academic world.

Highlights of Mosaic 1 Writing Silver Edition

Interacting with Others
Questions and topical quotes stimulate interest, activate prior knowledge, and launch the topic of the unit.

New design showcases compelling instructional photos to strengthen the educational experience.

2

Cooperation and Competition

Connecting to the Topic

1. When and why do you learn things easily?
2. What is almost impossible for you to learn?
3. Do you prefer to study alone or with others?

In This Chapter

Genre Focus: Information

Writing Product
A paragraph on cooperation or competition in learning

Writing Process
- Share ideas about learning.
- Read about Cooperative Learning.
- Conduct a survey about how other people learn.
- Use vocabulary and expressions for writing about advantages and disadvantages.
- Learn about paragraph unity and paragraph parts.

> **"** Talent wins games, but teamwork and intelligence win championships. **"**
>
> —Michael Jordan
> American basketball player–(1963—)

Making Use of Academic Content
Academic themes, activities, and writing topics prepare students for university life.

Activating Prior Knowledge
Chapter opening questions and pre-writing discussions activate prior knowledge and create a foundation for the writing activity.

Part 1 Preparing to Write

Getting Started

1 Talking About Some New Inventions Get together with a partner and look at these photos of technological innovations. Answer these questions:

1. What do you see?
2. How does it work?
3. What's your opinion of this innovation?

▲ An MP3 player

▲ Scientist using biotechnology to make genetically modified food

▲ Tiny handheld computer

▲ Using a GPS to drive

2 Brainstorming About the Usefulness of Technological Tools The photos show various examples of current or future technology. For each photo, list the way or ways this technological innovation makes life easier, more fun, or more convenient. Are there any disadvantages or problems with this innovation? Add that information. Then add more examples of current technological developments if you can. The first one is done as an example.

Innovation	How does this make life easier, more fun, or more convenient?	Are there any problems or "drawbacks" to this innovation? What are they?
Handheld computer	Able to check e-mail; looks cool	Expensive; easy to lose

3 Freewriting About a Future Innovation Write for 10 minutes about a current or future technological innovation. You can either explain how it works, make predictions about it, or discuss its advantages and/or disadvantages.

4 Preparing to Read You are going to read an article about tiny machines. Before you read, answer the following questions:

1. The article that you are going to read describes examples of nanotechnology. Nanotechnology refers to very tiny technological devices. Guess what these words with the prefix *nano* mean:

   nanorobots or nanobots
   nanocontractors (a contractor is a person who manages building projects)

2. Another word that you will see in this article is *molecular*, the adjective form of *molecule*. What is a molecule? How big is a molecule?

◄ DNA cubes and shapes like these (shown here as computer models) could become the building blocks for self-replicating nanofactories that would build anything and everything, from "smart" paper to cars and buildings.

Organizing Information
Graphic organizers provide tools for organizing information and ideas.

Part 2 Focusing on Words and Phrases

Writing About People We Admire

1 Practicing Useful Words and Expressions The following expressions will help you write about people you admire. Read the expressions and review their meaning in the examples. Then write a sentence of your own.

1. play an important role — He plays an important role in my life.

_____

2. set a good example — She sets a good example for others.

_____

3. have a lot of responsibilities — Since her father died, he has a lot of responsibilities.

_____

4. depend on (someone) — I depend on him for many things.

_____

5. is close to — She is close to her mother.

_____

6. gets together — The family gets together frequently.

_____

2 Reviewing Definitions Here are more words that can help you write with detail about people you admire. With a partner, match the words in the column on the left with one of the expressions on the right. Write the letter on the line. Then write a sentence for each word on a separate sheet of paper.

_____ **1.** personality	**a.** family member
_____ **2.** influence	**b.** commendable
_____ **3.** admirable	**c.** look up to
_____ **4.** relative	**d.** think about with high regard
_____ **5.** idolize	**e.** style of interacting with others
_____ **6.** respect	**f.** affect someone's thoughts or behavior

The Essay

New Points: Parts of an Essay
■ In an essay, the writer states a main idea and develops that idea in more than one paragraph by explaining, describing, comparing, retelling an event, or using a combination of these writing techniques.
■ An essay includes an introduction, the main discussion (the body), and a conclusion. The main idea for the entire essay is called the *thesis statement*.

STUDYING PARTS OF AN ESSAY
Look at the following diagram. It shows how parts of a paragraph relate to parts of an essay:

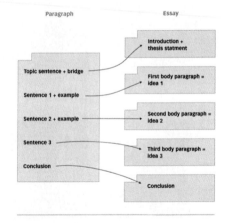

4. Complete Column II of the Gardner's Study of Great Leaders.

5. Does Julius Nyerere match Gardner's definition of a successful leader? Write your answer here and give at least one example. Share your answer and example(s) with your classmates when you are done.

_____

_____

Strategy

Thinking Critically: *Distinguishing Between General and Specific Information*

In the first reading, you read both general and specific information about great leaders. Understanding the difference between general and specific information is an important critical thinking skill. It is also helpful in learning to write well-developed paragraphs. Writers use specific information and examples to support general ideas.

7 Practicing Distinguishing Between General and Specific Information Look at the sentences below and on the next page and do the following:

- Insert > between the sentences if the sentence on the left is more general than the sentence on the right.
- Insert < between the sentences if the sentence on the left is more specific than the sentence on the right.
- Insert = between the sentences if they are equally general or specific.

The first one is done as an example.

A leader's story must be powerful.	>	Margaret Thatcher's message was an important part of her successful leadership.
Powerful stories help people discover where they are coming from.		Powerful stories help people discover where they are going.
Jean Monnet convinced French people as well as citizens and leaders of other nations that Europe did not have to remain a collection of hostile countries.		Jean Monnet's message was that there could be power, profit, and peace in dissolving or changing the boundaries.

TOEFL® iBT

Focus on Testing

Writing Introductions on Standardized Tests

In Part 3 of this chapter, you learned the importance of good paragraph and essay development, beginning with a good introduction. Writing effective, interesting introductions is a necessary part of any response in the writing section of the TOEFL® iBT.

- An introduction to either an independent prompt or an integrated prompt must do a lot of work:
- interest the raters
- lead the rater smoothly toward the main idea of your response
- show that your response is relevant to the task
- present a strong, clear thesis statement

A strong introduction is the first step toward a high score for any response.

Practice With one or two other students in your class, evaluate each of the following TOEFL® iBT-style introductions. Does it perform all four functions listed above? What are its strongest features? Its weakest ones? Finally, rank each introduction from 1 to 5, with the best introduction getting 5 and the weakest getting 1. Discuss your opinions with another group or with the rest of the class.

1. PROMPT: According to the reading and the lecture, how do socialists differ from Communists?

_____ INTRODUCTION: Socialists are very different from Communists. Both the reading and the lecture say so. Their differences are very interesting and form a very long list. Socialists have their beliefs and Communists have their own. Some socialist countries are Norway, Switzerland, and Yugoslavia. Some Communist countries are North Korea and Cuba.

2. PROMPT: Describe a situation in which you had to defend a friend against ill treatment by others.

_____ INTRODUCTION: Whenever my friend Gary walked into class, half the students in the class called him names like *Hairy Gary* or *Gary, the Human Ape*. Afraid to stand up for my friend, I sat silently, feeling sorry for him. I knew that Gary's long hair and unusual face made him look different from most kids, but I was his friend and I recognized his many talents. I was embarrassed by my unwillingness to speak out in his defense. That all changed in math class, the day before Thanksgiving 2003.

3. PROMPT: Explain how the lecture casts doubt on the information in the reading about robotics.

_____ INTRODUCTION: The reading about robotics makes several claims about the role of robotics in manufacturing. Movable "robot arms" do dangerous work like welding and riveting. Small, wheeled robots take care of tedious work like cleaning a warehouse floor, and tall, giraffe-like robots arrange products logically on shelves. And this is only a preview of more wondrous achievements to come. But does the lecturer take a similar position?

Scope and Sequence

Organizing and Developing Your Ideas	Critical Thinking	Focus on Testing	Evaluating Your Writing
■ The paragraph ■ The topic sentence	■ Recalling first impressions ■ Making inferences ■ Applying information questions in an interview ■ Analyzing paragraphs ■ Analyzing topic sentences	■ Focusing your paragraph	■ Rubric for writing an essay about first impressions ■ Self-assessment log
■ Paragraph unity ■ Paragraph parts	■ Comparing learning situations ■ Evaluating personal learning preferences ■ Considering advantages and disadvantages ■ Synthesizing information from a survey ■ Analyzing paragraph parts ■ Analyzing paragraph unity	TOEFL® iBT ■ Paragraph unity and a strong vocabulary	■ Rubric for writing an essay about cooperation or competition in learning ■ Self-assessment log
■ The essay ■ Studying parts of an essay ■ Building essays from paragraphs	■ Speculating about relationships ■ Making comparisons ■ Applying new information ■ Analyzing an essay ■ Developing an outline	TOEFL® iBT ■ Making an outline	■ Rubric for writing an essay about someone you admire ■ Self-assessment log

Organizing and Developing Your Ideas	Critical Thinking	Focus on Testing	Evaluating Your Writing
■ The thesis statement ■ Identifying types of supporting material ■ Organizing supporting material	■ Evaluating healthy/unhealthy choices ■ Comprehending a study of attitude and health ■ Analyzing sources ■ Applying new information ■ Synthesizing survey responses ■ Analyzing causes and effects ■ Analyzing thesis statements	**TOEFL® IBT** ■ Planning for writing on-demand	■ Rubric for writing an essay about personal aesthetics ■ Self-assessment log
■ Types of introductions ■ Well-developed para-graphs and essays ■ Sample essay: *Technology: size matters*	■ Comprehending a scientific article ■ Analyzing pros and cons ■ Analyzing word parts ■ Applying new information ■ Analyzing general and specific Ideas	**TOEFL® IBT** ■ Checking your main idea	■ Rubric for writing an essay about a technological innovation ■ Self-assessment log
■ Paragraph coherence through pronouns, key words, and paraphrasing ■ Conclusions	■ Identifying facts from the reading ■ Speculating ■ Making comparisons ■ Analyzing coherence ■ Applying new information	**TOEFL® IBT** ■ Conclusions on standardized tests	■ Rubric for writing an essay about success in business ■ Self-assessment log

Chapter	Writing Product	Preparing to Write	Focusing on Words and Phrases
7 Remarkable Individuals page 120	■ An **analysis** essay about a leader you admire	■ Talking about characteristics of a great leader ■ Brainstorming about great leaders ■ Freewriting ■ Readings: *Great leaders in the world* and *A great leader* ■ Gathering information: interview two people about leaders they admire	■ Vocabulary about leadership ■ Using word forms
8 Creativity page 140	■ A **definition** essay about a creative person or a creative product	■ Talking about creative people ■ Brainstorming about creative thinkers ■ Freewriting ■ Reading: *The creativity dance: advertisers use ideas from a choreographer* ■ Gathering information: research the result of creative thinking	■ Vocabulary about creativity ■ Expressions for making comparions

Organizing and Developing Your Ideas	Critical Thinking	Focus on Testing	Evaluating Your Writing
■ Ordering paragraphs in an essay ■ Supporting general ideas with specific information	■ Analyzing leadership ■ Organizing information from two reading selections ■ Distinguishing between general and specific information ■ Analyzing order in paragraphs ■ Predicting essay organization	**TOEFL® IBT** ■ Rubrics and writing tasks	■ Rubric for writing an essay about a leader you admire ■ Self-assessment log
■ Paragraph coherence through listing signals ■ Paragraph coherence through sentence connectors ■ Organizing a comparison paragraph	■ Analyzing creativity ■ Analyzing metaphors ■ Making comparisons ■ Analyzing paragraphs with sentence connectors ■ Recognizing organization patterns	**TOEFL® IBT** ■ Beyond *first, second, and third*	■ Rubric for writing an essay about a creative person or a creative project ■ Self-assessment log

Organizing and Developing Your Ideas	Critical Thinking	Focus on Testing	Evaluating Your Writing
■ Developing paragraphs with general to specific information ■ Practicing outlines ■ Sample essay: *Shau*	■ Interpreting expressions, gestures and body language ■ Analyzing and describing nonverbal messages and meanings ■ Recalling a sequence of events from reading ■ Interpreting what you read ■ Distinguishing fact from opinion ■ Sorting vocabulary ■ Analyzing sentence parts ■ Distinguishing between general and specfic points in a sentence	**TOEFL® IBT** ■ Writing introductions on standardized tests	■ Rubric for writing an essay about nonverbal behavior ■ Self-assessment log
■ Summarizing ■ Organizing a summary-and-reaction essay ■ Sample essay: *Berkeley coffee clash*	■ Generating different points of view ■ Identifying pro and con opinions ■ Recognizing provable statements ■ Analyzing key arguments in a debate ■ Developing counter arguments ■ Evaluating summaries	**TOEFL® IBT** ■ Citing sources for writing on standardized tests	■ Rubric for writing an essay about crime and punishment ■ Self-assessment log

New Challenges

In This Chapter

Genre Focus: Descriptive

Writing Product

A paragraph about your first impressions of a new place

Writing Process

- Describe photos of places around the world.
- Read some postcards of first impressions.
- Learn to make inferences.
- Interview someone who has traveled.
- Gather language for writing about impressions.
- Learn to write a paragraph and a topic sentence.
- Use a rubric to score your writing.

" First impressions are often the truest . . .**"**

——William Hazlitt
English writer and essayist (1778–1830)

Connecting to the Topic

1 Where are three places you've visited?

2 How did you get there?

3 When did you go?

Getting Started

 1 Talking About Postcard Photos The following postcard photos are from three big cities around the world. Describe what you see, and share your descriptions with your classmates. Have you visited any of these places?

▲ 1. Mexico City, Mexico

▲ 2. San Francisco, California, U.S.

▲ 3. Bangkok, Thailand

2 **Brainstorming About a Photo** Look again at the photos on page 4. Imagine a postcard photo from where you live now. Describe that photo. Then share your description with your classmates.

_____

_____

_____

_____

3 **Freewriting About First Impressions** Have you traveled to another city or country? Choose a place that you have visited. What were your first impressions? What was something that surprised you? What was different from your home? Think about sights, language, food, people, and transportation. Write for five minutes without stopping.

4 **Preparing to Read** Now read what your classmates wrote about the photos on page 4. Before you read, answer these questions in small groups.

1. Do you send postcards? When, and to which people?

2. Are first impressions always lasting impressions? Think of a first impression that changed.

5 **Reading** Read the postcards from around the world.

A Postcard from Thailand

> Bangkok, Thailand
> April 4
>
> Dear John,
> Wow—I have never seen so many motorcycles in one place! Almost everybody gets around on a motorbike. Everyone goes out in the evenings, too. I have visited two night markets. I bought lots of inexpensive souvenirs. There's no problem going out at night. It is very safe here. See you next week when I return.
> Kevin
>
> John Mercer
> 18 Placer Avenue
> San Bonita, CA 99763

A Postcard from San Francisco

North Beach (the Italian neighborhood!)
August 4

Dear Mom,
Almost everything in San Francisco is different than Boston. I'm glad I brought my jacket because the weather is cold and foggy. I am surprised that northern California is cold in August. The city is beautiful—there are lots of white buildings and hills. And there are so many different neighborhoods: Chinese, Japanese, Latino. Right now I'm sitting in an Italian coffee shop drinking a cappuccino. Tomorrow we'll visit Alcatraz!

Love, Teresa

Jeanne Nelson
1862 Third Street
Wichita, KS 67206

A Postcard from Mexico City

July 7

Ron,
I am having a great time visiting the museums here. I've learned so much about Frida Kahlo and Diego Rivera. I want to watch the movie Frida again. This city is perfect for visitors who love art. There is wonderful music at many of the restaurants. The food is delicious. I wish you were here, too. There is so much to see and do. Next time I'll bring you along!
I miss you!

Elena

Ron Anderson
2736 Threewhistle Way
Bayville, NY 11709

A Postcard from Tokyo

Tokyo
September 30

Hey Alex,
I've had lots of surprises since I arrived in Tokyo. The crowds are huge. There are many, many people everywhere. I get lost all the time. Luckily, everyone is very helpful and polite. Another surprise for me is the way restaurants show food in their windows. I don't have to read the menu. I can choose what I want to eat by pointing to the window display. That helps because my Japanese isn't very good—yet! I was also surprised to see that everything is neat and orderly. I like it here—it's wonderful.

Take care, David

Alex Fielding

16 Somerset Dr

Charlotte, NC 28202

▲ Tokyo, Japan

A Postcard from Istanbul

Istanbul
May 1

Hi Haluk—

   Istanbul is a beautiful city. It reminds me of San Francisco. My only problem is that everything is written in Turkish. Even though your father taught me a few Turkish expressions before I left, I can't remember anything. Nobody understands my poor pronunciation! People are friendly, and many of them speak English .I'm going to take a Turkish language class soon. I think things will get easier after that begins.

Ciao,
Pete

Haluk Boyko
729 Porter Place
Burlingame, CA 94010

 6 **Understanding What You Read** Answer these questions in small groups.

▲ Istanbul, Turkey

1. What does Kevin notice about Bangkok?

_____

_____

_____

2. What are two things Teresa notices about San Francisco?

_____

_____

_____

3. According to Elena, what kind of people would like Mexico City?

_____

_____

_____

4. What is going to improve for David?

_____

_____

_____

5. What is Pete's problem in Istanbul?

_____

_____

_____

Strategy

Thinking Critically: *Making Inferences*
You can use what you know from the postcards to make guesses about what you don't know. This is called *inferring*, and it is an important critical thinking skill.

7 **Practicing Making Inferences** Circle the number of the statement that you can infer from the information in the postcards you read. Explain your answers.

1. Boston is not cold in August.

2. It is expensive to visit museums in Mexico City.

3. Pete has visited San Francisco.

4. David does not speak Japanese.

5. There are no cars in Bangkok.

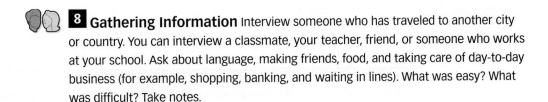 **8** **Gathering Information** Interview someone who has traveled to another city or country. You can interview a classmate, your teacher, friend, or someone who works at your school. Ask about language, making friends, food, and taking care of day-to-day business (for example, shopping, banking, and waiting in lines). What was easy? What was difficult? Take notes.

Visiting a New City or Country

Person's Name:
_____

City or Country Visited:
_____

Year:
_____

First Impressions:
_____
_____
_____
_____
_____

Difficulties:
_____
_____
_____
_____
_____

Part 2   Focusing on Words and Phrases

Describing Impressions of People, Places, and Things

1 Using Descriptive Adjectives The postcards from Part 1 include descriptive adjectives that describe first impressions.

In one of the postcards, David used descriptive adjectives and specific details to write about his first impressions of Tokyo. Review David's words in the chart on the next page. Then add some words and expressions about your first impression of a place using words from your Freewriting exercise in Part 1.

	People	Places	Things	Impression
David in Tokyo	helpful polite	crowded	wonderful	huge neat orderly
You in…				

 2 **Describing Problems** Study the following sentences that describe problems visiting a new place. Use them to write sentences, and then share them with a partner.

1. The *noun* is so *adjective*.
   The <u>weather</u> is so <u>cold</u>.

2. I'm having trouble with *noun*.
   I'm having trouble with <u>the language</u>.

3. I can't/You can't *verb*.
   I can't <u>remember new vocabulary</u>.

4. Many people *verb* here.
   Many people <u>use public transportation</u> here.

5. The biggest problem is *noun*.
   The biggest problem is <u>the high cost of everything</u>.

▲ Asking for directions

Asking and Answering Information Questions

Asking information questions is one way to learn about a new place and make new friends. These questions ask for more than a *yes* or *no* answer. Answers to information questions help you write about a new place.

3 Practicing Information Questions Make a list of information questions to ask someone who has visited another country. Write as many questions as you can for each question word. When you finish, share your list with your classmates.

1. What . . . ?

What were your first impressions?

_____

_____

_____

2. When . . . ?

When did the work day begin?

_____

_____

_____

3. Where . . . ?

Where can you find an Internet café?

_____

_____

_____

4. How much . . . ?

How much does it cost to take a bus tour of the city?

_____

_____

_____

5. How many . . . ?

How many people did you meet?

_____

_____

_____

6. How long . . . ?

How long does it take to fly there?

_____

_____

_____

7. Why . . . ?

Why did you visit this place?

_____

_____

_____

4 **Interviewing** Using your best information questions from Activity 3, interview someone about his or her experiences visiting a new place. You can interview the same person you worked with in Part 1, or you can find someone new. Write your questions and answers in the following chart.

Visiting a New Place

Person's Name:

_____

City or Country Visited:

_____

Year:

_____

Questions:

_____

_____

_____

_____

_____

Answers:

_____

_____

_____

_____

_____

5 **Listing Useful Words and Expressions** Make a list of words and expressions used to describe visiting a new place. If you need some ideas, look at the list of words and expressions in Activity 1 on page 11.

6 **Writing from Your Interview** Write about the person you interviewed. Describe his or her experiences in a new place. Use the information from your interview.

7 **Writing about Problems** Write four to six sentences about some problems you had visiting a new place. Use words and expressions you learned in this chapter.

8 **Writing about Good Things** Write four to six sentences about the positive things that you found in a new place. Use words and expressions you learned in this chapter.

Part 3 Organizing and Developing Your Ideas

The Paragraph

New Points: Paragraphs and Sentences
- A paragraph is a group of sentences that develops an idea.
- The sentences of a paragraph support and give examples of the main idea.
- Usually, a paragraph begins with an indented sentence.
- A paragraph can stand alone, or it can be grouped with other paragraphs to develop a more general idea, as in an essay.

DISCOVERING THE PARAGRAPH
This is a paragraph:

   You asked me to write about some of the things I've noticed that are new to me. The most striking thing is the huge crowds. There are many, many people everywhere, but everyone is very orderly and polite. People at home would not be so orderly in such crowds. Another new thing for me is the way restaurants display food in restaurant windows. They arrange it beautifully on lacquer trays in simple, clean designs. The Japanese seem to value the appearance of the food more than the taste. In my opinion, the sushi here is more delicious than at home.

How do you know it's a paragraph?
- The first sentence is indented.
- There is a main idea: All the sentences are about things David noticed in Tokyo.
- Each sentence is an example of something he has noticed.

This isn't a paragraph:

I went to the Grand Canyon this winter and to Mexico two years ago. I visited Taxco and bought some silver jewelry. The trip reminded me of vacations when I was young because my family always visited interesting tourist spots. I really like to travel to different countries. And if I know the language of the country I'm visiting, I enjoy myself more, of course. I studied Spanish in high school, and now I'm studying English. Some day I hope to visit Australia.

How do you know it isn't a paragraph?
- The first sentence is not indented.
- The sentences are about different topics: a trip to the Grand Canyon, a trip to Mexico, memories, travel, languages.
- There is no main idea.

New Points: Topic Sentences
- A paragraph usually begins with a sentence that expresses the main idea. This is the **topic sentence**.
- The topic sentence contains only one main idea and it tells the reader what the paragraph is about.
- The topic sentence can also appear in the middle or at the end of a paragraph.

DISCOVERING TOPIC SENTENCES

This is a topic sentence:

There are a few things that I've had trouble with since I arrived.

How do you know?
- It introduces one main idea: difficulties since David arrived in Japan.
- It tells the reader what the paragraph is about.

This isn't a topic sentence:

I went to the Grand Canyon this winter and to Mexico two years ago.

How do you know?
- The first sentence includes more than one main idea.
- It does not tell the reader what the paragraph is about.

Focus on Testing

Focusing Your Paragraph

You read guidelines for a good topic sentence in this section. When you write a timed essay, make sure you follow the topic sentence guidelines. A good topic sentence will focus and guide your writing and help you complete your essay in the given amount of time.

 1 **Recognizing Topic Sentences** Underline the topic sentences in the following three paragraphs. They discuss things you may want to know before visiting a new place: customs for touching, attitudes about beauty, and time. When you're finished, compare your answers with a classmate.

A. Generally, English speakers avoid body contact when they speak to each other. Sometimes they don't even shake hands. When they have to stand close together—for example, in an elevator—their muscles are tense, they avoid looking directly at each other, and they are silent. Even husbands and wives do not show affection in public.

B. Every culture defines beauty differently. Africans think plump women are attractive; Europeans believe thin women are beautiful. People in some cultures believe that tattoos are attractive. Others consider body piercing a sign of beauty. Brightly dyed hair is another style that many find pleasant looking.

C. Americans are very serious about time in social activities. This seems extreme to some foreigners. Many Americans, for example, believe that church services should start at exactly 11:00 A.M. and end by 12:00; they do not permit ministers to preach too long. School dances must end at 10:00 P.M., even though the boys and girls are having a wonderful time. Americans sometimes judge restaurants by the speed of their service, rather than the quality of their food.

 2 **Adding Topic Sentences** The following paragraphs need topic sentences. Read each paragraph, and choose the best topic sentence. Compare your answers with a partner's.

Example

In fact, people all over the world go to France just to sample the excellent cooking. French food is famous everywhere, and the ingredients are not that foreign. As a matter of fact, though many people have difficulty with the French language, they often know French food terms such as *quiche, croissant, paté,* and *soufflé.* Although people visiting France can have a difficult time speaking French or making friends, they rarely have difficulty with the food.

Topic sentence

1   Many visitors have problems adjusting to French culture.
2   Everyone understands French food terms.
③   Visitors to France have no problem adjusting to French cuisine.

A.   Eye contact is a sign of respect in North America. In introductions as well as in general conversations, speakers look directly at each other. However, most people become nervous if there is too much eye contact: This is called staring. When shaking hands, people shake firmly and briefly. The expression "He shakes hands like a dead fish" refers to a limp or weak handshake, a sign of a weak character.

Topic sentence

1   Direct eye contact is important during introductions in North America.
2   In North America, limp handshakes are a sign of weak character.
3   Direct eye contact and firm handshakes during introductions are customary in North America.

B.   Staying with a friendly family can help a visitor adjust to a new environment. A host family can teach the visitor about customs and family life and give information about social activities. Most importantly, the visitor can make friends with members of the family. Visitors who stay with families when they visit a new place are often lucky.
—Jim Leonard

Topic sentence

1   Arriving in a new place can be a confusing experience for a visitor.
2   Because being a visitor can sometimes be lonely and difficult, staying with a family can help the person get comfortable.
3   A host family can learn a great deal about foreign people and their cultures by offering hospitality to visitors.

C. The most common problem foreign students face in adjusting to a new culture is an "identity crisis." Foreign students must adapt their old selves to a new situation, and this can result in personality changes. They may have to play a different role in this new environment. The identity crisis occurs when the student has to consider who she or he really is. The process can be difficult, but if the student is aware of this problem, she or he can usually overcome it.

—Jerry Wilcox, James O'Driscoll, Nobleza Asuncion-Lande, and Cal Downs

Topic sentences

1 When people move between cultures, certain problems with adapting always occur.

2 There are many problems a foreign student faces when he or she leaves home, such as finding a place to live and learning the way around town.

3 People face problems throughout life, and a foreign student is no exception.

 3 Using Topic Sentences to Predict Read the following topic sentences. For each one, make a prediction: What will be in the rest of the paragraph? Make notes about your predictions. Then compare your notes with a partner's.

Example

Most people live for a long time in a new culture before they can relax and accept what they see around them.

The new culture is different. The foreigner is nervous and confused
at first. Examples: College registration is bureaucratic and complicated.
After awhile, people become used to things; they accept them
and see the positive aspects.

1. Some very funny things happened to me during my first few days in Seoul, but the most comical was our night in the restaurant.

_____

_____

_____

_____

2. There are advantages and disadvantages to visiting a foreign country.

_____

_____

_____

_____

3. Sometimes the first impressions you have of a new place change once you have adjusted to the differences.

_____

_____

_____

_____

4 **Writing Topic Sentences Before Writing a Paragraph** Write topic sentences for the following three paragraphs. You might want to highlight or take notes on the ideas before writing your topic sentence. Remember that good topic sentences:

- have one main idea.
- have a clear focus.
- tell the reader what the paragraph is about.

A. Topic sentence:

_____

_____

For example, North Americans do not maintain eye contact during a conversation; however, South Americans do. A North American usually meets the other person's eyes for a few seconds, looks away, and then back again. A South American looks directly into the other person's eyes and considers it impolite not to continue. Another difference is how they use hand movements while speaking. South Americans use many gestures. The North Americans use gestures only occasionally. North and South Americans are similar regarding distance between people speaking to each other. Unless it is a close friendship, the North and South American stand about two to three feet apart. It's often possible to know where a person comes from by studying his or her body language.

B. Topic sentence:

_____

_____

> They say that anywhere you go you can recognize where people come from simply by the way they walk. In general, Japanese people (women in particular) take small, quick steps. American guys often walk with swinging arms and a rolling pelvis. Italian men take long steps and are very observant as they walk.

C. Topic sentence:

_____

_____

> A common example is the gesture of waving farewell. In Italy, the palm of the hand is held toward the speaker and the fingers make the motion of drawing the departing person back. In Spain, the movement is the same, but the hand is held horizontally. In France, the palm is frequently held facing the departing person, and the movement of the hand appears to push the departing person on his way. Some scholars think that exposing one's palm indicates surrender, so perhaps the French form of farewell implies a reassurance of nonaggression. Americans are inclined to show the palm also and move the flattened hand from left to right.
>
> —Lawrence Wylie

5 **Writing Topic Sentences After Writing a Paragraph** You can write a topic sentence after you decide what your paragraph is about. For example, imagine that David has to write a paragraph about his first impressions of Tokyo. He wants to organize his ideas first, then write the topic sentence, and then write the paragraph. The following steps show you how to write a topic sentence this way, using David's letter as a model.

Step 1

Make a list of all your first impressions when you visited a new place. Look at David's list, and then make a list of your ideas.

David's list of impressions of Tokyo	**Your list of impressions of _____**
I read a few travel books about Japan before I went.	_____
People are always in a rush.	_____
Tokyo is so crowded.	_____
People are helpful and polite.	_____
Food is displayed in resturant windows.	_____

Step 2

Look through the list and identify ideas that are related. This will help you find the main idea of your paragraph.

Cross out any unrelated items.

David's list   **Your list**

I read a few travel books about Japan before I went.

_____

_____

People are always in a rush.
Tokyo is so crowded.
People are helpful and polite.

_____

_____

Food is displayed in restaurant windows.

_____

_____

Step 3

Now write a topic sentence that describes the main idea you found in Step 2.

David's topic sentence   **Your topic sentence**

I've had lots of surprises since I arrived in Tokyo.

_____

_____

_____

_____

_____

Step 4

Exchange papers with a partner. Does your partner's topic sentence have a main idea? Does it tell the reader what the paragraph is about? Correct your topic sentence if necessary.

Your topic sentence

_____

_____

_____

_____

_____

_____

Step 5

Now write your paragraph. Remember to include all the ideas that are related to your topic sentence. Include specific details and examples to explain the main idea.

David's final paragraph

    I've had lots of surprises since I arrived in Tokyo. The crowds are hugeThere are many, many people everywhere. Luckily, everyone is very helpful and polite. I get lost all the time. Another surprise for me is the way restaurants show food in windows. I don't have to read the menu. I can choose what I want to eat by pointing to the window display. That's good because my Japanese isn't very good—yet! I like it here. I was surprised to see that everything is neat and orderly.

Your final paragraph

_____

_____

_____

_____

_____

_____

_____

_____

_____

_____

_____

6 **Writing About Your First Impressions** Use what you've learned from this chapter to complete this assignment:

> Write a paragraph about your first impressions of another new place you have been. Make sure you have a good topic sentence. You can focus on any of these ideas:
>
> - things that surprised you
> - funny experiences
> - problems

Part 4 | Evaluating Your Writing

Use the rubric on the next page to score your writing. Read the rubric with your class, then give your writing a score. A classmate and a teacher will score your writing, also. If you score your paragraph with a 1 or a 2 and you want to revise and improve it, you can do it now or you can wait and do it after Chapter 3. When you revise, use the writing characteristics in the next highest level to guide your revision. For example, if your score is a 2, use the characteristics in the "Excellent—3" category to help you write a better paragraph.

Here are some tips on how to use the rubric. When you score your writing, pay attention to these five elements: ideas (**content**), the way you have ordered the ideas (**organization**), the words and phrases you have used, the kinds of sentences you have written (**vocabulary and sentence structure**), your **grammar** and your **spelling and punctuation**. (You won't pay attention to elements **not** on the rubric. For example, you won't pay attention to handwriting or font or length of writing.) When scoring, look for the closest match between your writing and a score point (and its description) on the rubric.

Rubric for Writing About First Impressions

Score	Writing Characteristics
3 **Excellent**	■ **Content:** Writing presents first impressions clearly and provides details to help the reader imagine the place. ■ **Organization:** Topic sentence is clear and impressions are described in an interesting way; ideas connect to the topic sentence. ■ **Language:** Vocabulary is specific and descriptive; sentence types are varied to keep the writing interesting. ■ **Grammar:** Subjects and verbs agree; there are very few common grammar problems (pronouns, articles and plurals) so the meaning is clear. ■ **Spelling and Mechanics:** Most words are spelled correctly, and punctuation is correct.
2 **Adequate**	■ **Content:** Writing presents first impressions, but they may be brief and the reader may have questions. ■ **Organization:** Paragraph includes a topic sentence; some ideas may not connect to the topic sentence. ■ **Language:** Vocabulary is clear; sentences are mostly the same type. ■ **Grammar:** Subjects and verbs mostly agree; common grammar problems (pronouns, articles, and plurals) are distracting. ■ **Spelling and Mechanics:** Has some distracting spelling and/or punctuation mistakes.
1 **Developing**	■ **Content:** Writing is too brief or does not present first impressions clearly or there may be too many (unrelated) impressions. ■ **Organization:** Paragraph ideas do not connect to the topic sentence, or there is no topic sentence. ■ **Language:** Vocabulary is limited and/or there are too many mistakes to understand and/or follow the ideas; sentences have mistakes. ■ **Grammar:** Has many common grammar problems (pronouns, articles, and plurals) that are confusing to the reader ■ **Spelling and Mechanics:** Has many distracting spelling and/or punctuation mistakes.

Self-Assessment Log

In this chapter, you worked through the following activities. How much did they help you become a better writer? Check *A lot, A little,* or *Not at all.*

	A lot	A little	Not at all
I read some postcards about first impressions.	❏	❏	❏
I learned to make inferences.	❏	❏	❏
I interviewed someone who has traveled.	❏	❏	❏
I used descriptive adjectives in my writing.	❏	❏	❏
I asked and answered information questions.	❏	❏	❏
I learned about paragraphs.	❏	❏	❏
I learned about topic sentences.	❏	❏	❏
I evaluated my first draft.	❏	❏	❏
I used a rubric to score my writing.	❏	❏	❏
(Add something) _____	❏	❏	❏

_____

Cooperation and Competition

❝ Talent wins games, but teamwork and intelligence win championships. ❞

—Michael Jordan
American basketball player (1963–)

Connecting to the Topic

1 When and why do you learn things easily?

2 What is almost impossible for you to learn?

3 Do you prefer to study alone or with others?

Getting Started

 1 Talking About Photos of People Learning These photos show people studying alone and in groups. In your opinion, which of these is most effective for learning? Why? Share your answers with a partner.

▲ Student studying alone

▲ Students studying together

▲ Students studying in a large group

▲ Students studying in a small group

2 **Brainstorming and Sharing Ideas About Learning** First, read the following statements. Circle *A* if you agree or *D* if you disagree. Add a sentence of your own. Then talk about your answers with a partner.

1. "I always want to be the best in my class. I'm a very competitive person. Competition helps me succeed."

   A   D

2. "I like to learn with one other student. I can ask questions, and we can help each other. I don't like to ask questions in front of the whole class."

   A   D

3. "It's fun and helpful to work in groups. I get to know my classmates better, and we all teach each other."

   A   D

4. "I am not comfortable working with other students. I prefer to work alone."

   A   D

5. Add your sentence here:

   _____

   _____

3 **Freewriting About How You Learn Best** Do you learn best working with one, two, three, or more students or by working alone? Write about this for five minutes.

4 **Preparing to Read** You are going to read about a way of learning in groups. Before you read, answer these questions:

1. When was the last time you worked with one or more students to complete an assignment? What was the assignment? How did you divide up the work? Did you like working with other students?

2. What are some good things about learning in groups?

How Do We Learn Best What We Need to Learn?

Cooperative Learning:	We sink or swim together.
Individual Learning:	We sink or swim alone.
Competitive Learning:	If I swim, then you must sink.
	If you swim, then I must sink.

A   Students are often asked to work together in class. Through "group work," they work in pairs, triads, or teams to do a research report, make a presentation, or complete a chapter review. One well-known approach to working in groups is called Cooperative Learning and it is used in classrooms ranging from kindergarten to university. Teachers who use Cooperative Learning believe that having students   5
work cooperatively, not individually or competitively, leads to greater success for all. These teachers believe that Cooperative Learning teaches students to "swim together" in mastering skills and knowledge. Guidelines for Cooperative Learning specify a clear task, a common goal, and time for the group to complete the task. In addition, each group member has a specific role and is required to work on the task equally. Having a role helps each group member to succeed. Cooperative Learning   10
teaches group members appropriate ways to help each other and encourages everyone to do his or her best work. The group receives recognition for successful completion of the activity and the individual gets credit for the information learned. Cooperative Learning provides students with positive experiences that not only teach them academic skills and knowledge, but also teach important social skills. Family, friends, and bosses are always looking for people who understand how to   15
live and work effectively with others, and Cooperative Learning teaches these skills.

Adapted from material by Jami Hanreddy

 6 **Understanding What You Read** Answer these questions in small groups.

1. At what ages can students work in Cooperative Learning groups?

2. What do teachers believe about Cooperative Learning?

3. What are three guidelines for Cooperative Learning?

4. What does *sink* mean? What does *swim* mean?

5. What social skills can students learn from a Cooperative Learning situation?

_____

6. Do you think that Cooperative Learning helps students learn? Why, or why not?

_____

> ## Strategy
>
> **Thinking Critically: _Considering Advantages and Disadvantages_**
> Thinking about the positive and negative aspects of an issue is an important critical thinking skill. These positive and negative aspects are often called _advantages_ and _disadvantages_. Making a list of advantages and disadvantages is helpful in forming an opinion.

 7 Considering Advantages and Disadvantages Use the following chart to list the advantages and disadvantages of working in groups. The articles on page 30 presented several advantages. Can you think of disadvantages? When you have finished, discuss your list with a classmate.

Advantages of Working in Groups	Disadvantages of Working in Groups

 8 Gathering Information Choose a statement from Activity 2 on page 29 that you agree with. Change it to a sentence expressing a general opinion about all students. Here's an example:

"Competition helps me succeed."   Competition helps students succeed.

Write your sentence at the top of the questionnaire on the next page. You are going to collect opinions from others (and practice your English) by interviewing five people about their opinion on this topic. Take notes so you can bring the results of your interviews to class.

Questionnaire

Statement (point of view): _____

_____

_____

	Person 1	Person 2	Person 3	Person 4	Person 5
Name					
Age					
Male/Female? (Circle one)	M F	M F	M F	M F	M F
Occupation (Student, teacher, etc.)					
Do you agree with the statement? Circle Y (Yes) or N (No)	N Y	N Y	N Y	N Y	N Y

Did the people you interviewed agree with you? Tell your classmates who you interviewed and what you learned.

Part 2 Focusing on Words and Phrases

Writing About Cooperation and Competition in Learning

1 **Practicing Useful Vocabulary** Match the words on the left from the article in Part I to their synonyms. Write the letter on the line. Then write five sentences using the words and synonyms.

_____ **1.** collaborative

_____ **2.** appropriate

_____ **3.** task

_____ **4.** master skills

_____ **5.** pairs

_____ **6.** independently

_____ **7.** results

_c_ **8.** triads

a. learn techniques

b. groups of two

c. groups of three

d. assignment

e. together

f. suitable

g. alone

h. outcomes

Your sentences:

1. _____
2. _____
3. _____
4. _____
5. _____

WRITING ABOUT POSITIVE AND NEGATIVE QUALITIES

The following verb expressions are useful in writing about positive and negative qualities. Review the list and study the example sentences.

Words and Expressions	Examples
allow (someone to do something)	Working independently *allows* Soji to stay up very late and finish his homework.
encourage (something)	Team projects *encourage* compromising.
enable (someone to do something)	Working in triads *enables* Marissa to ask her partners for help.
create (something)	Cooperative Learning *creates* problems for some students when they have to work with difficult classmates.
provide (something for someone)	Working together *provides* opportunities for students to get along with many different classmates.
promote (something)	Some educators think that Cooperative Learning *promotes* success for everyone.
prepare (someone for something)	Employers want schools to *prepare* students for work with different people.
teach (someone to do something)	Some believe that Cooperative Learning *teaches* students to "swim together" in mastering skills and knowledge.
prevent (someone from something)	Some people believe classroom lectures *prevent* students from learning to work together.
discourage (something)	Talking in class can *discourage* learning.

2 Writing About Advantages and Disadvantages Answer these questions with information about your preferences and experiences. Use the verbs from the chart on the previous page to help you write about positive and negative qualities.

1. Does working alone and independently enable you to learn more than working in a group?

   _____

2. How does working in groups promote social skills?

   _____

3. In your opinion, does working in a group teach something that you can't learn working alone?

   _____

4. How does working independently prepare you for the future?

   _____

5. How does working in a group prepare you for the future?

   _____

6. How does not doing homework prevent people from learning?

   _____

7. What can discourage you from wanting to work in a group?

   _____

3 Choosing Appropriate Words Choose an appropriate word to complete each of the sentences below.

advantages	competitively	encourages	teaches
collaboratively	enables	promote	together

1. Cooperative Learning is a teaching technique that _____ students to work _____ in groups toward a common goal.

2. When working _____, students work against each other to succeed.

3. Cooperative Learning _____ positive social behaviors.

4. Learning _____ is possible in any subject.

5. One study concludes that work-groups _____ motivation and enthusiasm.

6. Working in groups has lots of _____ for students.

7. Cooperative Learning _____ "team spirit."

4 **Writing a Paragraph About a Learning Environment** Where do you learn best? Which learning environment works best for you? Write a paragraph about where you learn best beginning with one of these: inside, outside, in silence, where there's noise. Explain why. (You may want to use your writing from the Freewriting exercise in Part 1.)

5 **Writing a Paragraph About a Positive Learning Experience** Write a paragraph about a positive learning experience you had recently. Did you participate in a group or work independently?

Part 3 Organizing and Developing Your Ideas

Paragraph Unity

Review Points
Every paragraph has a topic sentence.
The topic sentence tells the reader what the paragraph is about.

New Points: Paragraph Unity
A paragraph has unity when all of the sentences relate to and develop the topic sentence.
Ideas in a unified paragraph are easy to follow and understand.

1 **Identifying a Unified Paragraph** Read Paragraph A below and Paragraph B on the next page. Which one is a better example of a unified paragraph?

A. Cooperation is one of the most important things to learn, and my school gives us many opportunities to practice. Once you're out of school, you can't always work with the people you want to, so it's good to learn to cooperate with everyone. My teachers assign group projects so that we can learn to work together. In one of my classes, there is a "Unanimous Superior" rating for students who have learned well and cooperated with others while completing the assignment. Sometimes we don't get along with others in our group. If we argue, we'll never finish the project, so we learn to compromise. I believe that cooperation is the key for doing well in and out of school.

B. On a basketball team, you have to pass the ball instead of hogging it, and that's cooperation. One time in my math class, we had to do a group project in pairs. I really didn't like the person I was supposed to work with. My partner and I talked. We ended up doing the work, and we got a good grade. My goal right now is to cooperate with others even if I don't want to work with them. I will do my best.

Paragraph A is an example of a unified paragraph. The topic sentence tells the reader what the paragraph is about (cooperation is important and the school provides ways to learn it). Each sentence relates to the topic sentence.

Paragraph B isn't unified. Can you see why? In Paragraph B, the topic sentence suggests that the reader is going to read an explanation of cooperation. But the writer continues to describe a previous experience and then describe a goal. Though the topic of the paragraph is cooperation, the sentences do not directly relate to the topic sentence.

PARAGRAPH PARTS

- A paragraph is organized when all of the sentences follow a logical order. Related information should go together.
- There are many different ways to organize a paragraph. The order you choose usually depends on the topic of the paragraph and the purpose of your writing.

A well-organized paragraph looks like this:

Topic Sentence: States your main idea.
Bridge Sentence: Explains your topic sentence and/or connects it to your examples.
Explanation, Elaboration, Example Sentences: Develop and support the main idea.
Restatement: Returns to or restates the main idea.

2 **Identifying Parts of a Paragraph** For each of the paragraphs on the next page:

- underline the bridge sentence.
- put a wavy line under the sentences that explain, elaborate, or are examples.
- put a dotted line under the sentence that restates the main idea.

A. This year, I learned how to work together and cooperate in a group. Most of the time, I'm assigned to work with other students, and the students in my group haven't always been very easy to get along with. Eventually, I realized that if I try hard enough, our group will do well. I must be patient because it takes time. My teacher taught us that even when some members of the group don't get along, the goal is to complete the assignment. I'm glad I learned how to work with other students because I think I will have to do this a lot in the future.

B. The single greatest advantage of Cooperative Learning for language students is that they speak a lot. Working in groups really promotes language learning. Students studying a language learn to speak by speaking. In a traditional classroom, students speak one at a time, and the teacher speaks more than the students. In Cooperative Learning groups, many students get to speak at the same time. Cooperative Learning is great for language learning.

C. Several studies show that Cooperative Learning has many positive results. These studies are from universities around the world and in many subjects. Results show that Cooperative Learning increases student motivation to learn. It helps students complete a task and encourages a positive attitude toward the subject. It improves relationships between students and gives students better feelings about themselves. Overall, students get higher scores on tests and are better critical thinkers. Cooperative Learning has many advantages.

3 **Choosing Sentences that Support the Main Idea** Edit the following paragraphs. Find the main idea; then cross out any sentences that do not relate to it.

A. Some students do well in a competitive classroom. These students work hard to be better than other students. Participating in sports can make one competitive. Teachers create competition in learning by talking about the students with the highest scores. They also create competition by having students play games. Some teachers even give prizes to the winner. Prizes are expensive sometimes. Competition for some students can motivate them to learn more.

B. Students who prefer to work alone often have trouble concentrating when other students are nearby. They try to find quiet places to study. Coffee shops are noisy. They can study successfully in libraries, study rooms, or alone at home. Sometimes they use ear plugs to find quiet and to concentrate. They wear head phones to listen to music. These students do best when there are no distractions.

4 Writing a Paragraph from Notes Read the following notes from a class discussion about education at American universities. Then use the notes to write a well-organized paragraph with all the necessary elements: topic sentence, bridge (optional), examples, and restatement. Since the notes suggest more than one main idea, you must choose a unifying theme for your paragraph and eliminate all unrelated ideas. Feel free to add information based on your knowledge and experience. First, complete the outline below the notes to help you organize your ideas.

Notes

- *Students are very competitive at large U.S. universities.*
- *Professors have many tricks to prevent cheating.*
- *There's a high failure rate at large American universities.*
- *Professors sometimes switch exam questions at the last minute.*
- *Professors supply test booklets; students cannot use their own.*
- *Monitors patrol large exam halls.*
- *Students sit far away from each other.*
- *Cheating is a cause for dismissal from most U.S. universities.*
- *At large U.S. universities, you rarely see students discussing their grades with each other, sharing notes, or forming study groups.*
- *Extremely difficult introductory courses eliminate a certain percentage of students from the more popular majors.*

Topic sentence:

_____

_____

_____

_____

Bridge (optional):

_____

_____

_____

_____

Example 1:

_____

_____

_____

_____

Example 2:

_____

_____

_____

_____

Example 3:

_____

_____

_____

_____

Example 4:

_____

_____

_____

_____

Restatement:

_____

_____

_____

▲ Doing research on the Internet

TOEFL® IBT

Focus on Testing

Paragraph Unity and a Strong Vocabulary

Paragraph unity is very important in any writing on the TOEFL ® Internet-Based Test (iBT). Nicely unified paragraphs give the raters a positive impression of your response. Unifying a paragraph also gives you a chance to show that you have a strong English vocabulary.

By using several words or phrases that mean almost the same thing, you can give your response a fluid, natural tone. On the other hand, a response that unnecessarily uses the same word or phrase over and over seems disorganized and repetitive. Imagine that you have started a paragraph with this topic sentence:

Both the reading and the lecture point out that wind is a major factor in the spread of a wildfire.

You could build the paragraph with sentences that repeated the words *wildfire* and *wind*, but that would not sound very smooth. It might also make a rater think that you have a limited vocabulary. A better approach is to vary your expressions, as in this sample paragraph:

Both the reading and the lecture point out that wind is a major factor in the spread of a wildfire. Strong breezes might push the blaze eastward for some time and then suddenly change direction. Such sudden turnarounds are greatly feared by firefighters, who might be trapped by the shifting inferno. The lecture mentions that this unpredictable airflow is made worse by local pressure differences created by the fire itself. The reading describes extreme events called "firestorms," but the lecture says that very few true firestorms actually occur. To be truly a firestorm, a fire must be so intense that tornado-like gales actually suck objects into a low-pressure zone at the heart of the flames.

For the previous reading, notice the variety of words with similar meanings in the table below.

Wind	Wildfire
breezes	blaze
airflow	fire
tornado-like gales	inferno
	firestorms
	flames

Practice
Choose one of the items below and make a table with words that mean almost the same as each underlined word.

a. How does the lecture about <u>pets</u> cast doubt on the reading's opposition to the owning of animals as personal <u>property</u>?

b. Describe a situation in which <u>indecision</u> caused you to <u>miss</u> an <u>opportunity</u>.

c. What are the best ways to keep <u>athletics</u> from ruining a college's <u>academic</u> reputation?

d. The reading and the lecture define <u>global trade</u> in different ways. What are the <u>main</u> differences between the two?

Writing Product

5 **Writing About Cooperation or Competition in Learning** Use what you've learned from this chapter to complete this assignment:

> Write a paragraph on cooperation or competition in learning. Focus on advantages or disadvantages. Use the chart below to plan your topic:

I will write about	———— cooperation ———— competition	in learning (subject) ————————————
I will focus on	———— advantages ———— disadvantages	———————————— ————————————

Part 4 | Evaluating Your Writing

Use the following rubric to score your writing. Read the rubric with your class, and then give your writing a score. A classmate and a teacher will score your writing also and explain reasons for their scores. After scoring, you can revise and improve this paragraph, or you can wait and revise your writing after Chapter 3.

Rubric for Writing About Cooperation or Competition in Learning

Score	Writing Characteristics
3 **Excellent**	■ **Content:** Topic of writing is clear and advantages and disadvantages are completely developed; writing may include information, examples, anecdotes, and/or opinion to help the reader understand the writer's point of view. ■ **Organization:** Topic sentence is clear, and ideas are unified to explain advantages and disadvantages; paragraph parts are clear. ■ **Language:** Vocabulary is specific; sentence types are varied to keep the writing interesting. ■ **Grammar:** Subjects and verbs agree; there are very few common grammar problems (pronouns, articles, and plurals) so the meaning is clear. ■ **Spelling and Mechanics:** Most words are spelled correctly, and punctuation is correct.
2 **Adequate**	■ **Content:** Writing presents a topic and advantages and disadvantages. ■ **Organization:** Paragraph includes a topic sentence; most ideas relate to topic sentence; most parts of the paragraph are clear and/or present. ■ **Language:** Vocabulary is clear; sentences are mostly the same type. ■ **Grammar:** Subjects and verbs mostly agree; common grammar problems (pronouns, articles, and plurals) are distracting. ■ **Spelling and Mechanics:** Writing has some distracting spelling and/or punctuation mistakes.

1 Developing	<ul><li>**Content:** Writing does not present a topic clearly, or advantages and disadvantages may be unclear or incomplete.</li><li>**Organization:** Paragraph parts are missing or unclear; there are some missing sentences, or there are ideas that do not relate to the topic sentence.</li><li>**Language:** Vocabulary is not specific or correct and/or there are too many mistakes to understand and/or follow the ideas; sentences have mistakes.</li><li>**Grammar:** Writing has many common grammar problems (pronouns, articles and plurals) that are confusing to the reader.</li><li>**Spelling and Mechanics:** Writing has many distracting spelling and/or punctuation mistakes.</li></ul>

Self-Assessment Log

In this chapter, you worked through the following activities. How much did they help you become a better writer? Check *A lot, A little,* or *Not at all.*

	A lot	A little	Not at all
I talked about different ways to learn.	❏	❏	❏
I read about Cooperative Learning.	❏	❏	❏
I surveyed people about how they learn best.	❏	❏	❏
I practiced vocabulary and expressions			
– for writing about learning.			
– for writing about advantages and disadvantages.			
I learned about paragraph unity.	❏	❏	❏
I learned about paragraph parts.	❏	❏	❏
I evaluated my first draft.	❏	❏	❏
(Add something) _____	❏	❏	❏

_____

3

Relationships

In This Chapter

Genre Focus: Descriptive

Writing Product

An essay about a friend or family member you admire

Writing Process

- Read about an uncle-dad-neighbor.
- Learn how to make comparisons.
- Interview someone about a person she or he admires.
- Practice vocabulary for describing people.
- Expand paragraphs to essays.

"To love is to admire with the heart; to admire is to love with the mind.**"**

—Theophile Gautier
French poet, dramatist, novelist, journalist, and literary critic (1811–1872)

Connecting to the Topic

1 Why do we admire others?

2 Are there people in the world everyone admires?

3 What types of people do we tend to admire?

Getting Started

 1 **Talking About Relationships** These photos show individuals with people they admire. Guess the relationship of these people and talk about why you think one admires the other person. Work with a partner and share your guesses with the class.

▲ **1.** *The student admires his teacher because he is very skilled.*

▲ _____

▲ _____

▲ _____

2 **Brainstorming About People You Admire** Think of people you know and admire. List their names and write why you admire them.

1. _____
   _____

2. _____
   _____

3. _____
   _____

4. _____
   _____

5. _____
   _____

3 **Freewriting About Someone You Admire** Choose one person from your list in the Brainstorming activity, and write for five minutes about him or her. Describe how you know this person and why you admire him or her.

 4 **Preparing to Read** You are going to read an article by a young student who writes about someone he admires. Before you read, answer these questions in small groups.

1. What are three reasons we admire people?

2. Are there people in your life who are not family members but act as if they are?

My Uncle-Dad-Neighbor Larry

A   Everybody has somebody special, and for me it's Larry Williams. When I was only two years old, my parents were divorced. You can imagine how I felt: lost, abandoned, unwanted. However, there was someone across the street to help me. For many years, Larry has had a really important role in my life. He has been like my dad—the dad I never really had. Even today, I refer to him as my dad, and if somebody asks how my family knows him, we say he's my uncle. Larry and I are very close, and he's the man I most admire. 5

B   Larry owns his own construction company in the city called City Concrete, and because he has a lot of responsibilities, he works very hard. Before City Concrete, he worked in a science lab. You can see that someone 10 who can move from laboratory work to running a construction business is very smart. Larry is very smart. Construction is tough work, but he can always find time to get together with my family and me.

▲ Larry is a great role model

C   Larry loves science and history, and he wants to pass on his passions to me. When I go to his house, I don't just watch TV; we go to bookstores and he teaches me about topics like electricity and the Vietnam War. He is writing a book about science right now (I don't know the subject), and he hopes to get his book published. One weekend about a month ago, my best friend Nick and I went over to Larry's house. We talked, well, mostly listened, and learned about chemicals used to kill insects that eat plants. Some chemicals kill plants, too. Now he wants to teach me about geology and earthquakes.

D   Larry loves the outdoors more than almost anything and knows so much about nature. He is one of those guys who is outdoors every chance he gets. He has a huge telescope that he uses to teach me astronomy. He is constantly reading—sometimes about history, but mostly about science. On one of our "science weekends" he rented a very nice microscope, and we got to see single-cell animals moving around. Larry's so curious about the world.

E   I think Larry is the way he is because he grew up fishing and camping. When he was just a teenager, he was drafted into the army and sent to Vietnam as a photographer. He didn't have to fight, he just took and developed pictures. It's a good thing because he isn't the fighting kind of guy.

F   I am realizing now that many of Larry's interests are mine, too. Because of his influence, I think I will study biology when I get older. Larry has been a dad; I like to spend time with him and he is an inspiration for my future.

5 **Understanding What You Read** Answer these questions in small groups:

1. How do we "meet" Larry? How does the writer introduce him?

2. Which of these do we know about Larry?

_____ his age

_____ how he met the writer

_____ his marital status

_____ his work

_____ his interests

_____ how he spends his free time

_____ what he looks like

3. Why do you think the writer included certain information about Larry (but not everything he knows)? Which items in the list above are most important?

4. What are two reasons why the writer admires Larry?

5. Is there anyone in your life like Larry? Who? Describe this person.

Strategy

Thinking Critically: *Making Comparisons*
Comparing, pointing out similarities and differences, is an important critical thinking skill. Including comparisons in your writing will help you develop a description of a person you admire.

6 **Practicing Making Comparisons** Use the underlined words to write comparisons of your own based on those from "My Uncle-Dad-Neighbor Larry."

1. Larry <u>is like</u> my dad.

_____

2. Larry <u>loves</u> the outdoors <u>more than almost anything</u>.

_____

Share your comparisons with your classmates when you are finished.

7 **Gathering Information** Interview someone about a person he or she admires. Ask the person you interview to describe the person first and then to talk about why he or she admires this person. You will use the language and ideas from this interview for the writing assignment later in the chapter, so take notes.

Choose at least five questions from the list below. You can also make up your own.

Questions

- Name someone you admire. How do you know this person?
- What is your relationship to this person?
- What does this person look like?
- How does this person act?
- What is this person's work?
- Do you see this person often?
- Why do you admire this person?
- What are some examples that show why this person is admirable?
- How do you feel about this person?

An Interview with _____

Question 1: _____

Answer: _____

Question 2: _____

Answer: _____

Question 3: _____

Answer: _____

Question 4: _____

Answer: _____

Question 5: _____

Answer: _____

Writing About People We Admire

1 **Practicing Useful Words and Expressions** The following expressions will help you write about people you admire. Read the expressions and review their meaning in the examples. Then write a sentence of your own.

1. play an important role   He plays an important role in my life.

_____

2. set a good example   She sets a good example for others.

_____

3. have a lot of responsibilities   Since her father died, he has a lot of responsibilities.

_____

4. depend on (someone)   I depend on him for many things.

_____

5. is close to   She is close to her mother.

_____

6. get together   The family gets together frequently.

_____

2 **Reviewing Definitions** Here are more words that can help you write with detail about people you admire. With a partner, match the words in the column on the left with one of the expressions on the right. Write the letter on the line. Then write a sentence for each word on a separate sheet of paper.

_____ **1.** personality	**a.** family member
_____ **2.** influence	**b.** commendable
_____ **3.** admirable	**c.** look up to
_____ **4.** relative	**d.** think about with high regard
_____ **5.** idolize	**e.** style of interacting with others
_____ **6.** respect	**f.** affect someone's thoughts or behavior

3 Choosing the Correct Expression

Circle the word or phrase that best expresses the meaning of the underlined words in the five sentences below.

1. She is <u>close to</u> her aunt.

   a. is similar in size to
   b. is the same age as

   c. has a deep and loving relationship with
   d. was named for

2. She <u>idolized</u> her big sister when she was young.

   a. strongly admired
   b. didn't get along with

   c. looked like
   d. competed with

3. She and her mother <u>get along well</u>.

   a. have frequent disagreements
   b. enjoy each other's company

   c. go places together
   d. live close to each other

4. They <u>have a lot in common</u>.

   a. look alike
   b. are the same age

   c. share many interests
   d. own property

5. Her grandmother <u>depends on her</u>.

   a. expects her assistance
   b. hides from

   c. shares personal information with
   d. quarrels with

4 Writing a Paragraph About Someone Older or Younger

Write a paragraph about someone you admire who is older or younger than you are. Use the vocabulary you've learned in this section.

5 Writing a Paragraph Using Ideas from Freewriting

Write a paragraph about someone you admire using your ideas from the Freewriting activity on page 47.

▲ Younger siblings often admire older siblings.

From Paragraph to Essay

> **Review Points**
> - In a unified paragraph, all the sentences relate to and develop the topic sentence.
> - In an organized paragraph, all the sentences flow smoothly and are in a logical order.

In the first two chapters, you wrote paragraphs. Now you're going to learn how to expand a paragraph into an essay.

 1 Beginning with a Paragraph Read the following paragraph by a student about her older brother. Then answer the questions with a partner.

> When I think of someone I look up to, I think of my brother. Although my name for my brother shows respect and we are very attached to one another, our behavior doesn't always show that. My brother has very short brown hair because he's in the military. Before he went to training camp in San Diego, he helped me a lot with my homework. My brother didn't just help me with school, though. I respect and love my brother so much.
>
> —Cathy Lai

1. What is the main idea of the paragraph?

_____

2. How does the writer develop her main idea?

_____

3. In order to expand this paragraph into an essay, which points can the writer "expand"? Where can the writer provide more information?

_____

4. Does the paragraph seem unified to you? Organized?

_____

The Essay

> **New Points: Parts of an Essay**
> - In an essay, the writer states a main idea and develops that idea in more than one paragraph by explaining, describing, comparing, retelling an event, or using a combination of these writing techniques.
> - An essay includes an introduction, the main discussion (the body), and a conclusion. The main idea for the entire essay is called the *thesis statement*.

STUDYING PARTS OF AN ESSAY

Look at the following diagram. It shows how parts of a paragraph relate to parts of an essay:

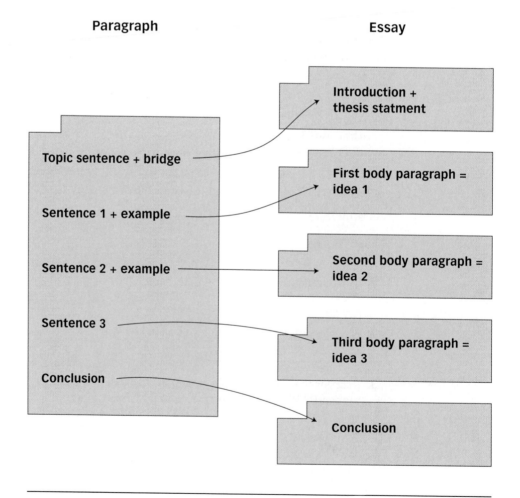

Paragraph

Essay

Topic sentence + bridge

Sentence 1 + example

Sentence 2 + example

Sentence 3

Conclusion

Introduction + thesis statment

First body paragraph = idea 1

Second body paragraph = idea 2

Third body paragraph = idea 3

Conclusion

2 **Expanding a Paragraph to an Essay** Now read how Cathy expanded her paragraph into an essay:

My Brother Joe

A   When I think of someone I look up to, I think of my brother. His name is Joe, but I never call him that. I always say "Brother" in Chinese because he is older than I am, and that is the way I show him respect. He calls me Cathy. Although my name for my brother shows respect and we are very attached to one another, our behavior doesn't always show that.   5

B   My brother has very short brown hair because he's in the military. His gold-framed glasses and small brown eyes go with his hair and give the impression that he's more organized, more efficient, and more serious than he really is. I used to see him every day, but now, since he joined the Marine Corps, I only see him on weekends. He always wears his uniform when I   10 see him now, and he sort of smells like corn starch.

C   Before he went to training camp in San Diego, he helped me a lot with my homework. Homework was hard for me because I was a slow learner. I wouldn't have passed many tests and quizzes without his help. And although my grades weren't as good as his, he was always proud of me when   15 I came home with passing scores. When we walked home from school together, he would always say, "Good job! Get the same grade next time or I'll beat you up!" Of course I said "No way!" and hit him. He'd hit me back, and we'd go running all the way home trying to catch each other.

D   When he left for training camp, I felt sort of empty. My brother doesn't   20 know it, but he taught me a valuable lesson by leaving. I had to work on my own and learn to be independent. I wish he were still living with us and bothering me like always. But by leaving, he showed me I can work by myself and still learn what I need to know to continue my education.

E   My brother didn't just help me with school, though. I remember one   25 summer when I was 10 and he was 17. The weather was unusually hot, and I started to feel itchy all over my body. I started to scratch. In no time, I got hives. Hives are these big bubbles on your skin. My brother helped me with so many things. He got me orange juice, lotion, and a spray bottle filled with water to stop the itching. He even bought me ice cream to cool   30 me down. He set up the fan to blow in my face and changed the channels on the TV for me. By the end of the day, the hives were almost gone. I said thanks to him. He said, "Shh! I'm watching something on TV." I threw a pillow at him and laughed.

F   My brother likes to act tough. He doesn't talk much and he seems very   35 serious, but I think he would do anything to help me. I respect and love my brother so much.

3 Writing an Outline Complete the following outline of the essay you just read, "My Brother Joe."

I. Introduction and thesis statement

_____

II. First idea

_____

III. Second idea

_____

IV. Third idea

_____

V. Fourth idea

_____

VI. Conclusion

_____

4 Comparing the Paragraph and the Essay Now compare the essay to Cathy Lai's original paragraph on page 53 and answer these questions.

1. What parts of the essay are the same as or similar to the paragraph?

_____

2. What parts of the essay are new?

_____

3. Where were these new parts added?

_____

4. Can you identify any of these new parts as: (a) description, (b) retelling an event, (c) comparing, (d) writing about feelings?

_____

5. Why were the new parts added?

_____

▲ Parents can make great role models.

5 **Building Essays from Paragraphs: No. 1** Expand this paragraph into an essay by completing the three steps that follow.

> My parents played an important role in my educational development by helping me in both material and spiritual ways to become the person that I am today. They raised my older brothers and sisters in such a way that they would set a good example for me and the other younger children. They bought various books that helped me become a hardworking student and a good reader. They also exposed me to experiences such as vacations and museum trips that enlarged my perspective on life. In addition, they looked carefully at my examination results in school in order to motivate me always to do my best. In short, I owe all of my positive qualities to the efforts of my parents.
>
> —Solomon Gebreaftse

Step 1 Make an outline in note form of the paragraph.

Write the topic sentence here:

_____

What is the first idea?

_____

What is the second idea?

_____

What is the third idea?

_____

What is the fourth idea?

_____

Step 2

Based on your experience and the reading you've done in this chapter, add supporting information to each of the ideas in Step 1. You can do this by giving a further explanation of what you think the writer means by each of his ideas. Use specific examples and details. Write your supporting points in the extra space provided under each idea in Step 1.

Step 3

Now write an essay based on your outline. Remember that the paragraphs, although part of an essay, should contain all the elements you've been practicing in the book up to this point.

▲ Three generations of a family

6 Building Essays from Paragraphs: No. 2 Here is another paragraph that you can expand into a complete essay. First, read the paragraph.

> My grandpa is very nice and very, very smart. We do lots of things to-gether, and I always learn a lot. He likes to play games with me, and he always wins. He is also a very good cook, so whenever I visit him, he makes delicious food. Sometimes my grandpa takes me out in his boat to fish or just to have a good time on the lake. He also likes to take me to the car mu-seum. I think I'm lucky to have a grandpa who likes to spend time with his grandson.
>
> —Aaron Marks

Now expand this paragraph into an essay by following Steps 1 through 3 from Activity 5. How many paragraphs will this essay have?

 7 Starting an Essay with Your Own Paragraph Write a paragraph about someone you admire.

Make an outline like the ones in Activities 3 and 5. Then expand your paragraph into an essay. Share your original paragraph, the outline, and the essay with a classmate before you give it to your teacher.

8 Expanding Your Paragraph to an Essay Expand one of the paragraphs you wrote in Chapter 1 or 2 into an essay. First, make an outline. Give the original paragraph, the outline, and the new essay to your teacher.

Focus on Testing

Activities 3, 5, 6, and 7 ask you to make an outline before you write your essay. An outline is a commonly used method for organizing ideas. Whenever you write an essay under time pressure, list the main ideas in an outline, and develop your supporting ideas from the outline. This will help you save time and keep your writing focused.

Writing Product

9 Writing About Someone You Admire Write an essay about the following topic:

> Write an essay about a friend or family member you admire. Use what you've learned from this chapter to complete the assignment.

Part 4 Evaluating Your Writing

Use the following rubric to score your writing. Read the rubric with your class, then give your writing a score. A classmate and a teacher will score your writing also and explain reasons for their scores. You can revise and improve this essay, or you can revise a paragraph from Chapter 1 or 2.

Rubric for Writing an Essay About Someone You Admire

Score	Writing Characteristics
3 **Excellent**	■ **Content:** Writing presents a person completely, and description includes information, accomplishment(s), anecdotes, comparisons, and/or dialogue to help the reader understand why this person is admirable. ■ **Organization:** Ideas are organized to support and explain how and why the writer admires someone; there is an introduction, body paragraphs, and a conclusion; ideas are connected to main idea. ■ **Language:** Vocabulary is specific and descriptive; sentences in each paragraph develop the topic sentence. ■ **Grammar:** Subjects and verbs agree; common grammar problems (pronouns, articles, and plurals) are minimal so that meaning is clear. ■ **Spelling and Mechanics:** Most words are spelled correctly, and punctuation is correct.
2 **Adequate**	■ **Content:** Writing presents a person, and description includes information that shows why he or she is admirable. ■ **Organization:** Ideas are organized into paragraphs, and there is a clear beginning, middle, and end. ■ **Language:** Vocabulary is descriptive; sentences are mostly the same type. ■ **Grammar:** Subjects and verbs mostly agree; common grammar problems (pronouns, articles, and plurals) are distracting. ■ **Spelling and Mechanics:** Writing has some distracting spelling and/or punctuation mistakes.

1 **Developing**	■ **Content:** Writing does not present a person clearly or does not develop description with sufficient details or explanation. ■ **Organization:** Not enough ideas to be an essay, or ideas are confusing. ■ **Language:** Vocabulary is limited or repeated and/or there are too many mistakes to understand and/or follow the ideas; sentences have mistakes. ■ **Grammar:** Writing has many common grammar problems (pronouns, articles, and plurals) that are confusing to the reader. ■ **Spelling and Mechanics:** Writing has many distracting spelling and/or punctuation mistakes.

Self-Assessment Log

In this chapter, you worked through the following activities. How much did they help you become a better writer? Check *A lot, A little,* or *Not at all.*

	A lot	A little	Not at all
I talked about why people admire others.	❏	❏	❏
I read an essay about an uncle-dad-neighbor.	❏	❏	❏
I learned to make comparisons.	❏	❏	❏
I interviewed someone about a person she or he admires.	❏	❏	❏
I studied vocabulary and expressions for describing people.	❏	❏	❏
I learned how to expand a paragraph into an essay.	❏	❏	❏
I evaluated my essay.	❏	❏	❏
(Add something) _____	❏	❏	❏

_____

4

Health and Leisure

In This Chapter

Genre Focus: Cause and Effect

Writing Product

An essay about activities that contribute to good health

Writing Process

- Talk about the relationship between daily habits and good health.
- Write about your habits and health.
- Read about cynicism and mistrust and health.
- Interview three people about their healthy (or unhealthy) habits.
- Practice vocabulary and expressions for writing about causes and effects.
- Learn to write a thesis statement.
- Practice spontaneous writing.

❝ To keep the body in good health is a duty . . . otherwise, we shall not be able to keep our mind strong and clear. **❞**

—Hindu Prince Gautama Siddharta
Founder of Buddhism (563–483 B.C.)

Connecting to the Topic

1 Do you consider yourself healthy?

2 What are three characteristics of good health?

3 What do you do to stay healthy?

Getting Started

 1 Talking About Everyday Activities and Health   The photos show people doing things that affect their health. What are the people doing in each photo? How does it affect their health? Share your answers with a partner.

▲ Photo 1

▲ Photo 2

▲ Photo 3

▲ Photo 4

2 Talking About Your Habits What do you do or not do that affects your health? With a partner, talk about what you eat or do or think about.

3 Brainstorming About Causes of Good and Bad Health Look at the photos on page 64 again. In small groups, talk about activities that can lead to good health or poor health. (Talk about both physical and mental health.) As you talk, jot down words and expressions that you use in one of the following columns.

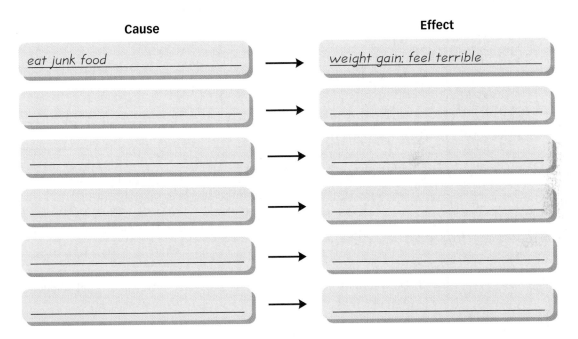

Cause	Effect
eat junk food	→ weight gain; feel terrible
	→
	→
	→
	→
	→

4 Freewriting about Your Habits and Your Health Write for seven minutes (without stopping) about your healthy (and unhealthy) habits. What kind of food do you eat? How often do you eat? How much exercise do you get? Write as much as you can.

▲ Do you try to eat healthy food?

5 Preparing to Read Many of us believe that working too hard and being very competitive (called "Type A personalities") can result in health problems. But what about frequent anger leading to health problems? Have you heard of that? The article you will read presents some new information about personality and health. Before you read, do the following activity.

Questionnaire

What kind of person are you? Take this quiz and discuss your answers with the class.

1. You are in the express checkout line (10 items or fewer) at the supermarket. The person in front of you has at least 15 items.

   a. How do you feel? _____

   b. What do you do? _____

2. You are looking for a parking place in a very crowded area. When you finally find a place, a driver behind you rushes in to take it.

   a. How do you feel? _____

   b. What do you do? _____

3. Do you think most people are basically honest?

   _____ Yes

   _____ No

4. How often do you yell at people who make you angry?

   _____ Never

   _____ Sometimes

   _____ Frequently

5. Cynical people are negative and distrustful about other people and their motivations. Are you cynical?

   _____ Yes

   _____ No

6. Have you ever hit someone because you were angry?

   _____ Yes

   _____ No

7. When something makes you angry, how long do you stay angry?

   _____

8. Do you feel that you have a lot of problems and disagreements in your everyday life?

   _____ Yes

   _____ No

Cynicism and Mistrust Tied to Early Death

A   A psychiatrist[1] has found that people who are angry and cynical are five times as likely to die under the age of 50 as people who are calm and trusting. This differs from what many researchers used to believe: that "Type A" people—people under stress who work too hard and are always in a hurry—were likely to die early from heart disease. The psychiatrist Dr. Redford B. Williams believes that his work disproves this theory. He feels that hostility[2], rather than stress, leads to premature[3] death.

B   During the 1970s, Dr. Meyer Friedman and Dr. Ray Rosenman, cardiologists[4] in San Francisco, identified "Type A" men. Type A men, according to the cardiologists, were twice as likely to suffer heart disease as relaxed men, a group that they labeled "Type B." However, a series of studies conducted in the early 1980s failed to prove that there was a connection between Type A personalities and heart problems. "We can now state with some confidence that of all the aspects that make up the Type A pattern, only those related to hostility and anger really lead to heart problems," Williams said.

C   Williams based his findings on numerous studies, including a 25-year study of 118 lawyers. The study participants took a standard personality test when they were in law school. Those who received high scores on hostility traits were five times as likely to die before age 50 as classmates who were not hostile. Personality traits such as paranoia ("People are picking on[5] me"), social avoidance ("I'd rather cross the street than meet that person"), and neurotic behaviors[6] were not related to early death. However, personality traits that reflected cynical mistrust ("People lie to get ahead"), anger, and angry behavior ("I often have to get rough with people") were strong predictors of premature death.

D   Cynicism and anger are expressed in everyday events, Williams said. For example, many people get annoyed or anxious when, in an express checkout line at the grocery store, other people have more than the allowed number of items. The angry personality type will not just feel upset, Williams said. He will act on his anger. Furthermore, angry people report more problems in their everyday lives, he said. Hostile and nonhostile people seem to have fundamentally different nervous systems, Williams said. When nonhostile people become upset, their nervous system acts like a "stop switch" that calms them down. Hostile people, on the other hand, seem to have weak nervous systems—they can't calm down. The levels of adrenaline[7] in their bodies remain high, and they stay unpleasantly aroused[8] and continue to feel angry, Williams said.

E   These differences appear in infancy[9]. When they become upset, hostile people also have larger rises in blood pressure than nonhostile people. This can lead to damage of the heart and blood vessels in hostile people. The hearts of calm, trusting people last longer, Williams claimed, because they are protected from the damage the nervous system can cause. "I think we should abandon[10] the Type A hypothesis," Williams stated. "There is no evidence that the Type A personality is likely to die young. But there is lots of evidence that people who are hostile and angry do."

—Sandra Blakeslee

1 psychiatrist = a doctor who studies, diagnoses, or treats mental illness
2 hostility = anger
3 premature = early
4 cardiologists = doctors who study, diagnose, or treat heart problems
5 pick on = treat unfairly
6 neurotic behavior = behaviors that are not exactly normal but are not the result of serious mental illness
7 adrenaline = a hormone
8 aroused = physically excited, in this case, by the hormone adrenaline
9 infancy = the state of being a baby
10 abandon = forget

6 **Understanding What You Read** Answer these questions in small groups.

1. What are two traits of "Type A" personalities?

_____

_____

_____

_____

2. According to Dr. Redmon, which is worse:

_____ working too hard

_____ being hostile

3. Which of these health problems do angry, cynical people tend to have?

_____ they're often nervous

_____ high blood pressure

_____ heart problems

_____ frequent headaches

_____ premature death

4. What did Friedman and Rosenman's series of studies prove?

_____ There is a connection between "Type A" personalities and health.

_____ There is no connection between "Type A" personalities and health.

_____ "Type A" personalities and "Type B" personalities are the same.

5. Think about three difficult scenarios (you can refer to the reading selection or describe your own scenarios). How do you think an angry, cynical person will react to these situations? How would a nonhostile person react?

Hostile Person	Nonhostile Person

6. Complete this sentence:

   Hostile people have _____ nervous systems because when they become upset, they can't calm down.

7. Do you know any hostile people? What do they do when they're upset?

8. In your opinion, is it possible for a person to change his or her basic personality characteristics?

Strategy

Thinking Critically: *Analyzing Sources*
Do you believe that anger can lead to early death? Is the Williams study of hostility traits from "Cynicism and Mistrust Tied to Early Death" convincing? Are there enough details about the study to convince you of Williams' conclusions? Analyzing the method of a study (how researchers arrive at the results) is a useful critical thinking skill. It's a good idea to consider how researchers arrive at their conclusions when you read research results.

 7 **Practicing Analyzing Sources** Use the following questions to help you analyze the Williams study in a small group.

1. Who conducted the study?

2. How much time was spent on the study?

3. How many people were in the study? What was their profession?

Are you convinced?

8 **Gathering Information** Do most people lead healthy lives? Interview three people about healthy or unhealthy choices they make. You can talk to classmates, teachers, family, friends, or people in your community. Use the chart below.

	Person 1	Person 2	Person 3
1. What is one thing you do every day to stay healthy?			
2. What is something you do that is not healthy?			
3. What do you do when you get upset?			
4. How important is good health to you? Choose a number. (1, 2, 3; 1 = very important)			

Part 2　Focusing on Words and Phrases

Writing about Health

1 **Reviewing Useful Expressions** The words and expressions in the column on the left are useful in writing about health. Find their synonyms on the right. Write the letter on the line. Check answers with a partner.

_____ **1.** lifestyle	**a.** surroundings
_____ **2.** calm	**b.** mental outlook
_____ **3.** stressed	**c.** annoyed
_____ **4.** attitude	**d.** regular habits
_____ **5.** angry	**e.** relaxed
_____ **6.** environment	**f.** tense
_i_ **7.** diet	**g.** physically fit
_____ **8.** active	**h.** out of shape
_____ **9.** inactive	**i.** what you eat

2 **Using New Vocabulary in Sentences** Write sentences using at least eight words or phrases from either column in Activity 1. Share your sentences with a partner or with the class.

3 **Writing About a Photograph** Write about one of the photos from Part 1 on page 64. Describe what people are doing. Use words and expressions from the chart. Share your writing with a partner.

4 **Writing About Your Habits** Write a paragraph about what you do, eat, or think about that affects your health. Use words and expressions from Activity 1 on page 70.

Showing Causes and Effects

WRITING ABOUT HEALTH USING CAUSES AND EFFECTS

When people write about health, they often discuss causes and effects. Review the following list of expressions for discussing causes and effects.

CAUSE		EFFECT
Noun	causes leads to results in contributes to has an effect on	noun
	Examples	
Daily exercise A lack of exercise	contributes to leads to	good health. obesity.

EFFECT		CAUSE
Noun	comes from results from is a result of is caused by	noun
	Examples	
A weak nervous system Lung cancer	is a result of is caused by	frequent anger. smoking.

5 **Matching Causes and Effects** Look at the chart below. On the right are some common health conditions, and on the left are causes for these conditions. Match each health condition with its cause. Some conditions may have more than one cause. Note the form of the nouns in the right column (some are noncount).

Causes	Common Health Conditions (= Effect)
_____ **1.** a nonhostile personality	**a.** excess weight
_____ **2.** a good diet	**b.** a long life
_____ **3.** overeating	**c.** heart disease
_____ **4.** exercise	**d.** strong muscles
_*e*_ **5.** anger	**e.** hypertension
_____ **6.** smoking	**f.** normal blood pressure
_____ **7.** relaxing	**g.** lung cancer
_____ **8.** stress	**h.** a healthy heart

6 **Writing Cause and Effect Sentences** Practice writing sentences using the above words and expressions with cause and effect expressions from page 71.

Example *A good diet results in a long life.*

▲ Do you eat enough fruit and vegetables?

7 Identifying Causes and Effects in a Paragraph Read the following paragraph about high blood pressure. Underline any cause and effect expressions. Then rewrite the paragraph. Replace each cause and effect expression with a new one from the list on page 71.

High blood pressure places a severe strain on the heart, blood vessels, and kidneys. That strain may eventually cause the heart to enlarge and become thickened. In some cases, the heart may fail. High blood pressure can also cause the blood vessels to "overstretch," weaken, or burst; a ruptured blood vessel in the brain can cause a stroke or even paralysis. The third and most serious complication related to high blood pressure is kidney failure. When the kidneys cease to function, they no longer filter out waste products. The result of kidney failure may be serious illness, or even death.

Part 3 Organizing and Developing Your Ideas

Review Points
- An academic essay includes an introduction with a thesis statement, the main discussion, and a conclusion.

New Points: Thesis Statment
- A thesis statement expresses the main idea of an essay.
- A thesis statement announces the topic and suggests the ways in which the writer will support his or her point of view.
- A thesis statement usually appears somewhere in the first paragraph of an essay. Most academic writers put it at the end of the first paragraph of an essay.
- A thesis statement can include two to four supporting ideas. You should be able to develop each supporting idea in one paragraph.
- Each supporting idea should have the same degree of generality; that is, don't put a general idea with a very specific one.

1 Answering Questions About Thesis Statements Here is a thesis statement from an essay about how lifestyle affects health. Answer the questions.

A positive mental attitude, regular exercise, and a well-balanced diet are all aspects of a lifestyle that contribute to good health.

1. Find the part of the thesis statement that states the topic of the essay and underline it.

2. Find the ideas in the thesis that support the topic. How many are there?

_____

3. Suppose that this thesis statement is the answer to a question. Which question does the thesis statement answer?

_____ How is a person's lifestyle affected by the weather?

_____ What are some factors that contribute to good health?

_____ What is a well-balanced diet?

4. Based on this thesis statement, what do you predict the writer will say? Which of these questions do you think the writer will answer?

_____ How is a person's lifestyle affected by the weather?

_____ Why does regular exercise lead to good health?

_____ How can a well-balanced diet make a person feel good?

_____ What is a positive mental attitude?

_____ What is the old food pyramid?

_____ How can a positive mental attitude contribute to good health?

▲ Regular exercise contributes to good health.

5. Choose why this is not a good thesis statement:

> **People can do many things in their daily lives to be healthy.**

_____ This thesis statement announces the topic, but the reader doesn't know what the supporting ideas are.

_____ This thesis statement only gives the supporting ideas.

(Yes, as you probably noticed, this thesis statement is missing an important part: the supporting ideas, so the first reason is correct.)

2 **Recognizing Good Supporting Ideas** When you write thesis statements, you want to make sure that the supporting ideas have the same degree of generality. Which of the following thesis statements are weak because the supporting ideas are unequal?

1. The Hunzukuts' longevity is due to heredity and lifestyle.

_____ Good _____ Needs rewriting

2. The Hunzukuts' longevity is due to heredity and the fact that they don't smoke.

_____ Good _____ Needs rewriting

3. Research has shown that people will live longer if they avoid stress and don't eat sugar.

_____ Good _____ Needs rewriting

3 **Recognizing Strong and Weak Thesis Statements** Read the following thesis statements and decide which ones are good examples and which are not. Use the New Points about Thesis Statements on page 73 to help you decide. Rewrite each weak thesis statement. Work with a partner. The first one is done for you.

1. College education prepares you for a successful future.

_____ Good __*X*__ Needs rewriting

By taking practical courses, making lifelong friends, and learning life skills, college education prepares you for a successful future.

2. People from different cultures have different diets.

_____ Good _____ Needs rewriting

3. There are many popular books on maintaining good health and losing weight.

_____ Good _____ Needs rewriting

Focus on Testing

Planning for Writing On-Demand

Whenever you have to write an essay under time pressure, planning your time before you take the test will reduce your stress and help you write more confidently. Make a schedule according to these guidelines:

For 20 percent of the time allotted: Read the topic, underline important words and phrases.

For 40 percent of the time allotted: Plan your response. Make an outline or do a graphic organizer to get your ideas down and in order.

For 40 percent of the time allotted: Write.

Practicing On-Demand Writing

Some exams give students only a very short amount of time to write an essay. It's good to be able to write a thesis statement quickly that answers the question. Practice this. Read the questions and write a thesis statement. Work quickly: imagine that you are taking a real test.

1. Should science and technology students have to take communication skills courses in college?

   _____

2. What are the major differences between your culture and another culture?

   _____

3. What is success?

   _____

4. What are some differences between young people today and young people in the past?

   _____

5. What are the main causes of poor health among college students?

   _____

6. When is competition productive?

   _____

7. What can a college student learn about life outside of the classroom?

   _____

8. What are some of some disadvantages of living in a crowded urban area?

   _____

5 **Reviewing Thesis Statements with a Classmate** When you finish Activity 4, compare your thesis statements with a partner's. How are they similar? How are they different?

Writing Product

6 **Writing About Causes of Good Health** Use what you've learned in this chapter to complete this assignment:

> Write an essay about what people can eat, do, or think about that contributes to good health. Focus on cause and effect, a good thesis statement, and the vocabulary and expressions you learned.

▲ Running is a great, inexpensive form of exercise.

Use the following rubric to score your writing. Read the rubric with your class, and then give your writing a score. A classmate and a teacher will score your writing also and explain reasons for their scores. You can revise and improve this essay, or you can wait and revise it after Chapter 6.

Rubric for Writing an Essay About Causes of Good Health

Score	Writing Characteristics
3 **Excellent**	■ **Content:** Writing presents two or more causes of good health and explanation includes facts, examples, anecdotes, and/or personal experiences that are convincing. ■ **Organization:** Essay begins with engaging introduction and clear thesis statement; ideas are organized in paragraphs with topic sentences that support and explain causes of good health; conclusion reminds the reader of the purpose of the essay. ■ **Language:** Vocabulary and expressions effectively show causes and results; sentence types are varied and keep the reader interested. ■ **Grammar:** Subjects and verbs agree; common grammar problems (pronouns, articles, and plurals) are minimal so that meaning is clear. ■ **Spelling and Mechanics:** Most words are spelled correctly and punctuation is correct.
2 **Adequate**	■ **Content:** Writing presents one or two causes of good health, and explanation includes facts, examples, anecdotes, and/or personal experience. ■ **Organization:** Thesis statement, body paragraphs, and conclusion are present but may be brief or confusing; reader has questions. ■ **Language:** Vocabulary and expressions show causes; there may be some misused words or expressions. ■ **Grammar:** Subjects and verbs mostly agree; common grammar problems (pronouns, articles, and plurals) are distracting. ■ **Spelling and Mechanics:** Writing has some distracting spelling and/or punctuation mistakes.

1 **Developing**	■ **Content:** Writing does not present causes clearly or does not develop explanation sufficiently. ■ **Organization:** Main idea may be unclear or missing; supporting ideas are unclear or too brief; writing may be a paragraph instead of an essay. ■ **Language:** Vocabulary is limited and/or there are too many mistakes to understand and/or follow the ideas; sentences have mistakes. ■ **Grammar:** Writing has many common grammar problems (pronouns, articles, and plurals) that are confusing to the reader. ■ **Spelling and Mechanics:** Writing has many distracting spelling and/or punctuation mistakes.

Self-Assessment Log

In this chapter, you worked through the following activities. How much did they help you become a better writer? Check *A lot, A little,* or *Not at all.*

	A lot	A little	Not at all
I talked about the relationship between daily habits and good health.	❏	❏	❏
I wrote about my habits and health.	❏	❏	❏
I read about cynicism and mistrust.	❏	❏	❏
I interviewed three people about their healthy (or unhealthy) habits.	❏	❏	❏
I studied vocabulary and expressions for writing about causes and effects.	❏	❏	❏
I learned how to write a thesis statement.	❏	❏	❏
I practiced spontaneous writing.	❏	❏	❏
I evaluated my essay.	❏	❏	❏
(Add something) _____	❏	❏	❏

_____

5

High Tech, Low Tech

In This Chapter

Genre Focus: Information

Writing Product

An essay about a future invention

Writing Process

- Read an article about nanotechnology.
- Research a recent technological innovation.
- Review vocabulary for writing about technology.
- Learn how to use direct quotations to support your opinion.
- Learn how to use paraphrases.
- Learn about several types of introductions.

"The best way to predict the future is to invent it."

—Alan Kay
American computer scientist (1940–)

1. What is the most useful "gadget" you own?

2. Which new technological invention would make a difference in everyone's life?

3. How has technology made your life different from your parents' life?

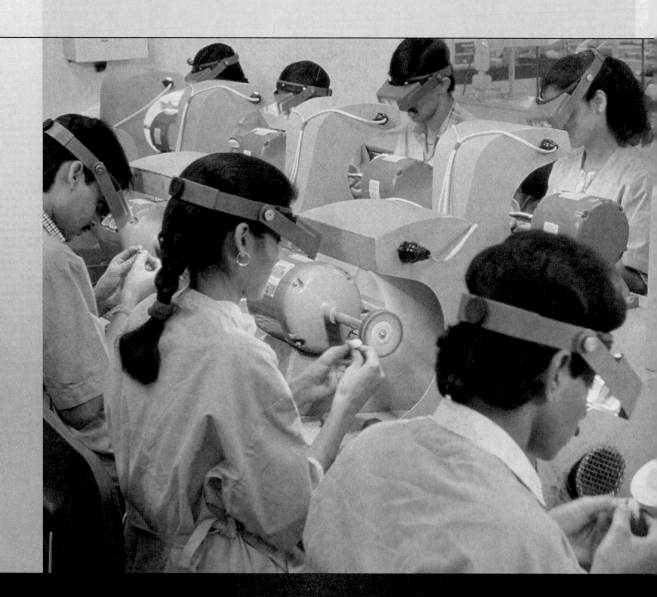

Getting Started

 1 **Talking About Some New Inventions** Get together with a partner and look at these photos of technological innovations. Answer these questions:

1. What do you see?
2. How does it work?
3. What's your opinion of this innovation?

▲ An MP3 player

▲ Scientist using biotechnology to make genetically modified food

▲ Tiny handheld computer

▲ Using a GPS to drive

2 Brainstorming About the Usefulness of Technological Tools The photos show various examples of current or future technology. For each photo, list the way or ways this technological innovation makes life easier, more fun, or more convenient. Are there any disadvantages or problems with this innovation? Add that information. Then add more examples of current technological developments if you can. The first one is done as an example.

Innovation	How does this make life easier, more fun, or more convenient?	Are there any problems or "drawbacks" to this innovation? What are they?
Handheld computer	*Able to check e-mail; looks cool*	*Expensive; easy to lose*

3 Freewriting About a Future Innovation Write for 10 minutes about a current or future technological innovation. You can either explain how it works, make predictions about it, or discuss its advantages and/or disadvantages.

4 Preparing to Read You are going to read an article about tiny machines. Before you read, answer the following questions:

1. The article that you are going to read describes examples of nanotechnology. Nanotechnology refers to very tiny technological devices. Guess what these words with the prefix *nano* mean:

   nanorobots or nanobots
   nanocontractors (a contractor is a person who manages building projects)

2. Another word that you will see in this article is *molecular*, the adjective form of *molecule*. What is a molecule? How big is a molecule?

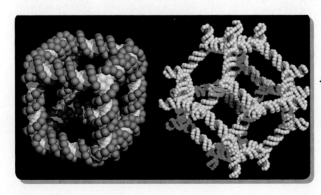

◄ DNA cubes and shapes like these (shown here as computer models) could become the building blocks for self-replicating nanofactories that would build anything and everything, from "smart" paper to cars and buildings.

Nanotechnology: The Science of the Small
by Noah Robischon

A   Imagine a microscopic assembly line.[1] Cubes made from DNA travel along a conveyor belt[2] made of cilia, the tiny hairs on the surface of cells. Along the way, robotic arms insert individual molecules into the cube: each molecule builds on the last. This entire micromanufacturing plant fits into a modern printer. It pushes out sheets of white paper. These sheets weigh as much as a regular piece of paper. However, each fiber of the paper is actually a tiny robot with a built-in memory equal to a Pentium Pro microchip. You ask the sheet of paper for information about the earthquake of 2054. It turns itself on, like a super high-definition television screen, and shows you a documentary on the subject.   10

B   You stop the program and search for details on how San Francisco was rebuilt after the disaster. It tells you that a team of architects, physicists, and chemists worked together; they created a workforce of nanocontractors, micromechanical robots that were programmed with architectural designs. A handful of these tiny robots, a few billion, were thrown onto the crumbled remains[3] of an old building. Some of the robots broke down[4] the existing raw materials—dirt, concrete, metal—into molecular parts. Another set of nanobots used these parts to construct the walls and windows of new buildings. This scene may seem like it came from a science fiction novel, but micromachines are already present in our everyday lives.   20 For example, a tiny accelerometer[5] in your automobile senses a crash and

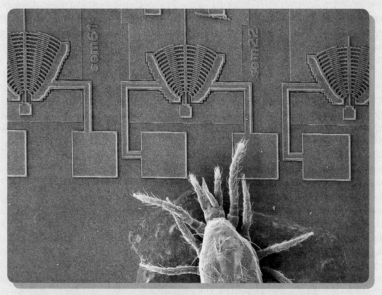

▲ A spider mite, which is not visible to the human eye, crawls across a part used in a micromachine manufactured by Sandia National Laboratories.

activates the air bags. Hospitals use tiny disposable microsensors to monitor patients' blood pressure from inside their veins. Products such as these not only exist today, but they're even getting smaller.

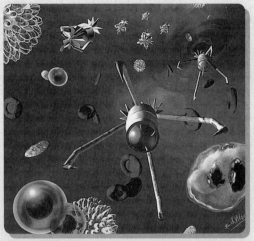

▲ Future applications of nanotechnology could include tiny molecular robots that swim through your bloodstream and fight disease.

C   In the next seven years, "Things will get wild[6]," predicts Bill Spence, editor of NanoTechnology magazine. "In 15 years, all of a sudden there will be no more automobile workers, just car designers." In Spence's future, auto workers will be replaced by robotic molecular assemblers[7].

D   At least one company, Zyvex, is already working on the molecular assembler. James R. Von Ehr II, the founder of the company, admits, however, that it isn't easy to be the first with a new technology. He believes that the first molecular assembler will be incredibly difficult to build. But if people build it correctly, he thinks the assembler will also be a replicator, capable of reproducing a thousand copies of itself.

D   Many scientists criticize Spence and people like him. "No one knows how to make those things yet; maybe some day, somebody will. But I don't think those guys will," says Dr. Julius Rebek, director of the Skaggs Institute. Rebek has been experimenting with self-assembling molecules for years and says, "Right now, there's no obvious way to do it." Spence may be overoptimistic, but nanotechnology is advancing rapidly, and the next breakthrough could come from anywhere—several Japanese electronics corporations are already busy working on similar technologies.

E   Wherever the breakthrough[8] does come from, one thing is clear: Big things often come from small particles. Future applications of nanotechnology could include tiny molecular robots that swim through your bloodstream and fight diseases.

---

1 assembly line = people or machines that work in a line to put parts together in a factory
2 a conveyor belt = a machine that moves parts along an assembly line
3 the crumbled remains = the broken bits and pieces of something that was destroyed
4 broke down = separated and organized
5 accelerometer = a machine that senses movement
6 get wild = become extreme or unusual
7 assemblers = people or machines that put things together
8 breakthrough = an innovation; a new thing or idea

5 **Understanding What You Read** Answer these questions in small groups.

1. What do you think the writer's purpose was in this reading selection? Check all that apply:

    _____ give information about a new technology

    _____ argue against a new technology

    _____ make predictions about a new technology

    _____ discuss the advantages and disadvantages of a new technology

    _____ argue for a new technology

2. In the beginning of the article, the writer describes an imagined scene from the future. What is happening in the scene?

3. Give an example from the article of a micromachine that is "present in our everyday lives," and describe how it works.

    _____

4. What prediction do you learn about in the article?

    _____

5. Some difficult terms are defined in the article. Find the definitions and write them below:

    cilia = _____

    raw materials = _____

    a replicator = _____

6. What is an example of an innovation being developed?

    _____

7. Does the author have positive or negative feelings about nanotechnology? Find examples in the article to support your answer.

    _____

8. What is your opinion of nanotechnology?

    _____

6 **Gathering Information** Do research on a future technological innovation that interests you. You can choose a gadget, object, or process. Think about a technological innovation that is not widely available yet but that may be available soon. Find information about your topic by interviewing someone who knows about this topic, by searching on the Internet, or by referring to the *Reader's Guide to Periodicals* at the library. Take notes in the chart below.

Here are some ideas for topics:

- Online learning
- Robots
- Genetic engineering

- Genetically modified food
- Space travel
- Multiuse handheld devices

Questions	Answers
What is the innovation?	
How is it used?	
What does it look like?	
How does it work?	
How does it make life easier?	
Are there any drawbacks to this innovation?	
Additional questions you can add:	

Strategy

Thinking Critically: *Analyzing Pros and Cons*
You learned in Chapter 2 about advantages and disadvantages. The advantages of a situation are called the *pros*. The disadvantages are called the *cons*. Considering the pros and cons of a technological innovation helps you be objective. Being objective is an important critical thinking skill.

7 **Practicing Analyzing Pros and Cons** Consider the pros and cons of the innovation you researched in the Gathering Information activity on page 87. Write down the pros and cons, and then present all of the information you found to the class. Use a chart like this:

Technological Innovation: _____		
	Pros	**Cons**
1.	_____	_____
2.	_____	_____
3.	_____	_____
4.	_____	_____
5.	_____	_____

Part 2   Focusing on Words and Phrases

Discussing Technology

 1 **Using Word Parts** You have noted that many words useful in discussing technological innovations have the same prefixes. *Prefixes* appear at the beginning of a word and carry meaning. Complete the following activities to learn some useful words and word parts when discussing technology. Work with a partner.

> **List 1**
> micromachines _____
> microsensors _____
> microscope _____
> a micromanufacturing plant _____
> microchip _____

    1. These words are (circle the correct answer):   nouns   verbs   adjectives

    2. What does the prefix *micro* mean? _____

    3. Guess the definitions of the words in List 1 and write them beside each word.

List 2

microscopic _____

micromechanical _____

microelectrical _____

4. These words are (circle the correct answer):   nouns   verbs   adjectives

5. Guess the definitions of the words in List 2 and write them beside each word.

List 3

nanotechnology _____

nanorobot _____

nanobot _____

nanocontractor _____

6. These words are (circle the correct answer):   nouns   verbs   adjectives

7. What does the prefix *nano* mean? _____

8. Guess the definitions of the words in List 3 and write them beside each word.

2 **Practicing Vocabulary and Expressions to Write About Technology**
Match the words on the left with their definitions on the right.

_____ **1.** optimistic	**a.** disadvantage
_____ **2.** innovation	**b.** something new
_____ **3.** drawback	**c.** saves money
_____ **4.** economical	**d.** feeling positive about something

3 **Writing a Paragraph About a Technological Innovation** Write a
paragraph in which you describe one of the photos in *Getting Started* on page 82.
Use some of the words and expressions from this section.

Strategy

Thinking Critically: *Using Direct Quotations to Support Your Opinion*
A good way to share information and support your opinions is to refer to the work
and ideas of others who have relevant experience and/or expertise. When you use
someone else's exact words, you must place all of them inside quotation marks
("...") and you must name the person who said or wrote them.

Example
"No one knows how to make those things yet; maybe some day, somebody will.
But I don't think those guys will," says Dr. Julius Rebek, director of the Skaggs
Institute.

4 **Answering Questions About Direct Quotations** Re-read the following paragraph from the article "Nanotechnology: The Science of the Small." Then answer the questions.

> In the next seven years, "Things will get wild," predicts Bill Spence, editor of *NanoTechnology* magazine. "In 15 years, all of a sudden there will be no more automobile workers, just car designers."

1. Who is being quoted? (Who is the source?)

_____

2. What are the qualifications of the person who was quoted? (Is he an expert? Where does he work? What does he do?)

_____

3. Is he explaining, predicting, or discussing an advantage or a disadvantage of nanotechnology?

_____

4. Why do you think the author chose to quote this particular passage?

_____

WAYS TO USE QUOTATIONS

Here are three ways to use quotations in your writing:

1. *According to* [name + qualifications] + quoted words
Examples
According to Nadrian Seeman, a structural chemist at New York University, "Biology is nanotechnology that works already."

2. Quoted words + *said, stated, claimed, predicted,* etc. [name + qualifications], . . .
Examples
"Biology is nanotechnology that works already," said Nadrian Seeman, a structural chemist at New York University.

3. [Name + qualifications] *said, stated, claimed, predicted [that]* . . .
Examples
Nadrian Seeman, a structural chemist at New York University stated, "Biology is nanotechnology that works already."

Follow these tips when using quotations:

- Use a quotation when you cannot say it better than the expert does.
- Follow these punctuation rules for quotations:
  - Put opening ["] and closing ["] quotation marks around all the words that you are quoting.
  - Use a comma between the words: *According to [name],* or *[name] said,* or *[name] stated* and the quoted material.

- Capitalize the first letter of the first word of the quotation.
- If the end of the quotation comes at the end of the sentence, put the period inside the last quotation mark.

Look at this example:

According to Samuel Greengard, "Automobile manufacturers soon will begin using tiny devices that run on static electricity to sense when to release an airbag and how to keep engines and brakes operating efficiently."

---

5 Writing Quotations Correctly Correct the punctuation in the following quotations.

1. According to Diane McAfee, Assistant Principal of Sunnyside Elementary School, "connecting schools to the Internet is just a fad".

2. Dr. Maryanne Volpe, of the Hamilton University biology department, stated We just don't know the long-term effects of genetically modified food.

3. According to Dr. Linda Eastman "there's no scientific proof that cell phones cause brain cancer."

4. Children spend too much time on the Internet and not enough time playing out doors said child psychologist Mark Evans.

5. In the future, computers will work with us, outside of us, and also inside of us, Dr. La Clair predicts.

PARAPHRASING TO SUPPORT YOUR OPINION

A second way to share information and support your ideas is to paraphrase other people's ideas. A paraphrase is a restatement of a phrase or sentence that is approximately as long as the original statement. (It's still important to say whose idea it is.) A paraphrase should be mostly your own words, but you can occasionally use the author's exact words if she or he has used a specialized or technical term, especially if there's no synonym.

Look at this example:

Quotation: "Genetic engineering of plants will produce 'supercrops' in the near future, such as short corn stalks loaded with ears, which will help end world hunger."

—Source: A study done by *The Branson Research Group*.

Paraphrase: A study conducted by The Branson Research Group predicts that genetic engineering will produce superior food crops that will someday abolish world hunger.

Notice these things:

- Some of the language from the original quotation was repeated. There's only one term for *genetic engineering*, there's no adequate synonym for *produce* in this context, and there's no other way to say *world hunger*.

- The corn example was not included. In developing an idea, if you need a concrete detail and your original source contains one, use it. If you want to save space or time by using a paraphrase, you can do so by omitting some of the details the source contains.

- The paraphrase includes the source of the information; if it's a reliable source, it helps support your argument.

Here are some tips for using paraphrases:

- Paraphrase when it is more effective or efficient to restate the author's words in your words.

- Don't forget to cite the source in a paraphrase.

- If you want to save time or space by using a paraphrase, omit some of the details.

- Use a dictionary or thesaurus to find words with similar meanings.

---

6 Practicing Paraphrases Write paraphrases for the following quotations about issues in technology. Refer to the preceding guidelines. Don't forget to cite the sources.

1. Quotation: "Routine, repetitive, and dreary blue-collar materials-handling jobs can be filled by robots for less than the minimum hourly wage."
   Source: The Copely News Service

2. Quotation: "A program at the Defense Advanced Research Projects Agency (DARPA) is developing computers capable of symbolic reasoning with effective computational speeds thousands of times greater than those used in military systems." (Note: Agencies, titles, or programs are like technical terminology—you can't paraphrase them.)
   Source: Robert Cooper, Director of DARPA

3. Quotation: "It's now possible to develop computers that are a billion times smaller than the typical desktop of today. They will be so small they can be woven into your clothing or spread on the wall embedded in paint."
   Source: Hewlett-Packard computer architect Philip Kuekes

7 Write a Paragraph About a Technological Innovation Use one quotation and at least one paraphrase; try to use some of the vocabulary from the lists in Activity 1, pages 88–89. Base your writing on the ideas and sources from your research from the Gathering Information activity on page 87.

Part 3   Organizing and Developing Your Ideas

Introductions

Review Points
- A thesis statement expresses the main idea of an essay.

New Points
- An essay begins with an introduction, which is usually the first paragraph.
- Its purpose is to prepare the reader for the essay.
- The introduction usually includes the thesis statement.

TYPES OF INTRODUCTIONS

There are several types of introductions: general-to-specific, definition/explanation, setting the scene, and problem-solution.

General-to-Specific

This type of introduction consists of two or three (or more) sentences that lead to the thesis, with each new sentence more specific than the previous one. This kind of introduction can be represented by an upside-down triangle:

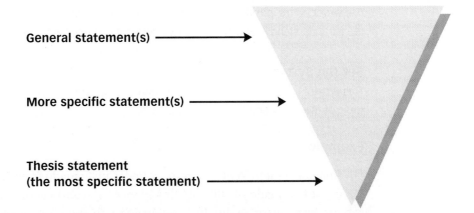

General statement(s) ⟶

More specific statement(s) ⟶

Thesis statement
(the most specific statement) ⟶

Example

A current trend in elementary education is networked classrooms. Schools everywhere are purchasing sophisticated computers and connecting to the Internet. Many schools have adopted a technology-based curriculum and are providing special training in the use of educational technology for teachers. Technology in education has important benefits for both students and teachers.

This introduction leads the reader on an increasingly narrow path to the specific thesis statement.

Definition/Explanation

This type of introduction prepares the reader for an informative essay that uses new terms or concepts. The writer defines or explains the new terms or concepts in the introduction so that the reader will understand the rest of the material in the essay.

Example

Nanotechnology is the science of the small. Derived from the Greek word for "dwarf," nano is a one-billionth unit of measurement. So a nanometer is a billionth of a meter, and a virus is nearly 100 nanometers across. Nanotechnology is the term used to describe a wide array of theoretical and experimental approaches to engineering tiny machines: everything from making smaller microchips, to envisioning molecular robots that could swim through our bloodstream and fight disease. People working in the field of nanotechnology today are divided between two disciplines: those working from the "bottom up," mostly chemists attempting to create structure by connecting molecules; and those working from the "top down," engineers taking existing devices, such as transistors, and making them smaller.

The writer of this introduction has defined nanotechnology, given examples to help the reader understand it, and explained two different approaches to the field.

Set the Scene

This type of introduction describes a scenario or incident to engage the reader in the topic of the essay and lead to the main idea.

Example

Imagine a microscopic assembly line. Cubes made from DNA travel along a conveyor belt made of cilia, the tiny hairs on the surface of cells. Along the way, robotic arms insert individual molecules into the cube: each molecule builds on the last. This entire micromanufacturing plant fits into a modern printer. It pushes out sheets of white paper. These sheets weigh as much as a regular piece of paper. However, each fiber of the paper is actually a tiny robot with a built-in memory equal to a Pentium Pro microchip. You ask the sheet of paper for information about the earthquake of 2054. It turns itself on, like a super high-definition television screen, and shows you a documentary on the subject.

You stop the program and search for details on how San Francisco was rebuilt after the disaster. It tells you that a team of architects, physicists, and chemists worked together; they created a workforce of nanocontractors, micro-mechanical robots that were programmed with architectural designs. A handful of these tiny robots, a few billion, were thrown onto the crumbled remains of an old building. Some of the robots broke down the existing raw materials—dirt, concrete, metal—into molecular parts. Another set of nanobots used these parts to construct the walls and windows of new buildings. This scene may seem like it came from a science fiction novel, but micromachines are already present in our everyday lives. For example, a tiny accelerometer in your automobile senses a crash and activates the air bags. Hospitals use tiny disposable microsensors to monitor patients' blood pressure from inside their veins. Products such as these not only exist today, but they're even getting smaller.

This long introduction (which you recognize from the reading selection in Part 1) describes an example of nanotechnology in vivid detail to introduce the reader to the subject of the essay and make a new or abstract topic familiar and concrete.

Problem-Solution

This kind of introduction begins with a short explanation of a problem, one that the essay will attempt to solve. The introduction ends with a solution to the problem.

Example

A recent study has shown that children watch an average of seven hours of television a day. This is a great concern to many parents. They worry that the violence on television will influence their children's behavior. They also worry that the frequent commercials for unhealthy food will affect their children's eating habits. Parents are, furthermore, concerned that television programs present false information that could be detrimental. What can they do? The solution to this problem is simple: Parents should carefully select the programs their children watch and limit the number of viewing hours.

Note that sometimes types of introductions overlap. That is, an introduction might have the characteristics of more than one of the types described in this chapter.

1 **Practicing Introductions** Write an introduction for one of the following thesis statements. Use one of the types discussed previously, or combine them. In your introduction, use your own ideas and opinions.

a. Everyday life has become more convenient for everyone through technological innovations.

b. The personal computer has helped me become a better student in two ways: I can do thorough, up-to-the minute research for my projects and papers, and I can produce professional-looking documents that are easy for professors to read.

2 **Rewriting an Old Introduction** Rewrite the introductory paragraph from one of your previous essays. Use an introduction presented in this chapter.

Essay Development

Review Points

- Readers should be able to predict what an essay is about from the thesis statement.
- The thesis statement can also include ideas the writer will use to support his or her viewpoint.

New Points: Essay Development

- A well-developed essay has concrete, relevant details.
- Supporting paragraphs should be balanced: they should contain information of equal importance presented in equal depth.
- Ideas should flow smoothly from one paragraph to another through well-chosen transitions.

3 **Answering Questions About Essay Construction** Read the essay on the next page about a kind of technology and then answer the questions.

Technology: Size Matters

A   Nanotechnology is the science of the small. Derived from the Greek word for "dwarf," nano is a one-billionth unit of measurement. So a nanometer is a billionth of a meter, and a virus is nearly 100 nanometers across. Nanotechnology is the term used to describe a wide array of theoretical and experimental approaches to engineering tiny machines: everything 5 from making smaller microchips, to envisioning molecular robots that could swim through our bloodstream and fight disease. People working in the field of nanotechnology today are divided between two disciplines: those working from the "bottom up," mostly chemists attempting to create structure by connecting molecules; and those working from the "top 10 down," engineers taking existing devices, such as transistors, and making them smaller.

B   Top-down, or mechanical nanotechnology, will have the greatest impact on our everyday lives in the near future. Cornell is one of five nanotechnology facilities in the country funded by the National Science Foundation. Re- 15 searchers from IBM, AT&T, and Raytheon are working on projects such as the disposable medical laboratory on a chip. This invention would allow a medical technician to place a drop of blood on a five-dollar chip, measuring the width of a dime, and connect it to a computer that would immediately process a diagnosis. Such a device is "no more than a few years away," says 20 Dr. Lynne Rathbun, the program manager at Cornell.

C   Perhaps less immediately useful, but equally important is the work being done by bottom-up scientists such as Nadrian Seeman, a structural chemist at New York University. Inspired in 1980 by an M.C. Escher drawing, Seeman used DNA to create a cube just seven nanometers across. Now 25 he's making more complex and stronger structures, such as truncated octahedrons that could be used to make new materials. He's even built a chemical switch that could potentially be used in a nanosized electronic device such as a bio-computer chip.

D   Seeman's work is influenced by biology more than engineering. "Biol- 30 ogy is nanotechnology that works already," Seeman says. Photosynthesis is, after all, a molecular-scale mechanical operation, and enzymes are essentially nanosize factories. The challenge for nanotechnologists is learning to control such processes. Once they do, huge advances in everything from microelectronics to chemical engineering will be possible. 35

1. Look at the thesis statement. On the basis of the statement, what do you expect to read about in the essay?

   _____

2. How do you expect the essay to be organized? That is, how many paragraphs do you predict, and what will be the subject of each paragraph?

   _____

3. What are the supporting ideas in the thesis? Write them here.

   _____

   _____

4. Are the supporting ideas balanced? That is, are they equally important? Are they of equal depth, that is, do they go into about the same amount of detail?

   Yes _____ No _____

5. Now, review the rest of the essay. How does the writer move from one paragraph to another? Are there transitions between paragraphs? How does the writer transition?

   _____

6. Make a list of some details that the writer includes in the body paragraphs.

   _____

   Are they concrete?
   Yes _____ No _____
   Are they relevant? (Do they all relate to the topic?)
   Yes _____ No _____

4 **Practicing Introductions** The following is a beginning draft of an essay about the advantages and disadvantages of technology. The draft is missing specific details. Rewrite the introductory paragraph. Make sure to include a thesis statement. Then complete the essay, making sure your paragraphs contain ideas that support and expand on your thesis statement.

> Technology is around us every day. We see examples of technology at home, where we work, where we study, and even where we play. Although technology has brought us many useful things, such as improved living conditions, it has also brought us disadvantages, such as air pollution.
>
> As a result of technological innovation, our living conditions have improved dramatically . . .
>
> Air pollution is one of the negative results of advanced technology . . .

Hint: Correct the thesis statement first. You may also want to make the transitions between paragraphs smoother.

Focus on Testing

Checking Your Main Idea

In questions 1 and 2 in the previous activity, you reviewed the thesis statement and predicted what the essay would be about. Whenever you write under time pressure, it is a good idea to go back to the beginning and check your thesis statement before you have completed the essay. Did you discuss what the thesis statement promised? Checking your main idea will help you write a coherent essay.

Writing Product

5 **Writing About Technological Innovation** Use what you've learned from this chapter to complete this assignment:

> Write an essay about a current or future technological innovation. Use new vocabulary and expressions learned in this chapter. Try one of the introduction types. Develop your ideas by using information from the research that you did in Part 1.

▲ A satellite dish

Part 4 | Evaluating Your Writing

Use the following rubric to score your writing. Read the rubric with your class, and then give your writing a score. A classmate and a teacher will score your writing also and explain reasons for their scores. After scoring, you can revise and improve this essay or you can wait and revise something you've written after Chapter 6.

Rubric for Writing About a Technological Innovation

Score	Writing Characteristics
3 **Excellent**	■ **Content:** Writing presents a current or future innovation and includes concrete, relevant details that are informative and interesting. ■ **Organization:** Introduction engages reader and leads to main idea (thesis statement); supporting ideas are organized in paragraphs that have smooth transitions from one to another; there is a conclusion. ■ **Language:** Vocabulary and expressions explain and describe technological innovation; new or abstract terms are defined; writing includes quotations or paraphrases to be convincing. ■ **Grammar:** Subjects and verbs agree; common grammar problems (pronouns, articles, and plurals) are minimal so that meaning is clear. ■ **Spelling and Mechanics:** Most words are spelled correctly and punctuation is correct.
2 **Adequate**	■ **Content:** Writing presents a technological innovation and includes some details. ■ **Organization:** Introduction includes a thesis statement; essay has a middle and end; some information may be missing; reader may have questions. ■ **Language:** Vocabulary and expressions describe topic; paraphrases or quotations may be misused. ■ **Grammar:** Subjects and verbs mostly agree; common grammar problems (pronouns, articles, and plurals) are distracting. ■ **Spelling and Mechanics:** Writing has some distracting spelling and/or punctuation mistakes.

1 **Developing**	■ **Content:** Writing does not present or develop a technological innovation clearly or sufficiently. ■ **Organization:** Main idea may be unclear or missing; supporting ideas and details are unclear or too brief. ■ **Language:** Vocabulary is limited and/or there are too many mistakes; difficult to understand the ideas; sentences have mistakes. ■ **Grammar:** Writing has many common grammar problems (pronouns, articles, and plurals) that are confusing to the reader. ■ **Spelling and Mechanics:** Writing has many distracting spelling and/or punctuation mistakes.

Self-Assessment Log

In this chapter, you worked through the following activities. How much did they help you become a better writer? Check *A Lot, A Little,* or *Not at all.*

	A lot	A little	Not at all
I talked about technological innovations.	❏	❏	❏
I read an article about nanotechnology.	❏	❏	❏
I researched a recent technological innovation.	❏	❏	❏
I reviewed vocabulary for writing about technology.	❏	❏	❏
I learned how to use direct quotations to support my opinion.	❏	❏	❏
I learned how to use paraphrases.	❏	❏	❏
I learned how to improve essay development through the use of details, balanced ideas, and transitions.	❏	❏	❏
(Add something) _____	❏	❏	❏

_____

6

Money Matters

In This Chapter

Genre Focus: Analysis

Writing Product

An essay about what leads to success in business

Writing Process

- Talk about successful businesses.
- Freewrite about what leads to success in business.
- Read an article about a successful business.
- Research a successful business.
- Study business vocabulary.
- Practice writing coherent paragraphs.
- Learn about conclusions.

❝ Success in business requires training and discipline
and hard work. But if you're not frightened by these
things, the opportunities are just as great today as they
ever were. **❞**

—David Rockefeller
American banker (1915–)

Connecting to the Topic

1 Which successful business company would you like to join?

2 What are some ways businesses can be successful in addition to making lots of money?

3 What aspect of business interests you the most?

Getting Started

1 **Talking About Some Successful Businesses** Following are names of some successful businesses. In small groups, answer the following questions. If you don't know, make a guess.

- What do you know about these businesses, their products, or their services?
- Why are these businesses successful?
- What does a business need to do or have in order to be successful?
- Why do some businesses fail?

▲ The Body Shop, a body-care products company that strives to be a model of social and environmental responsibility

▲ Sony Corporation revolutionized personal electronics with the transistor radio and the Walkman.

▲ ebay is a very successful web-based company. It is an electronic auction trading platform.

2 **Brainstorming About Successful Businesses** In small groups, think of three other successful businesses you know about. Complete the chart on the next page. For each company, list the name of the company; the product(s); why the company is successful, in your opinion; and whether you think it will continue to be successful.

Name of Company or Business	Product	Why Is It Successful?	Will It Remain Successful?	Why?
Starbucks	coffee	• good marketing • located everywhere • new drinks frequently	Yes	• People will always want coffee. • The drinks are familiar and addictive.

3 **Freewriting About Business Success** What leads to success in business? Describe what you consider to be a typical successful business. Write for five minutes without stopping. To get started, use some of the ideas you discussed in the Brainstorming activity on page 104.

4 **Preparing to Read** You are going to read an article about a new approach to success in business in Korea. First, discuss your answers to these questions in small groups.

1. Before you read, review the meanings and pronunciation of these words related to *entrepreneurship.* Look them up in a dictionary, if necessary.

Nouns
entrepreneur (a person)
entrepreneurship
enterprise (a business)

Adjectives
entrepreneurial
enterprising

---

2. Discuss the economy (use of time, money, resources) in your country right now. Are companies making large profits, or are many companies losing money? Does everyone who wants to work have a good job, or is there a lot of unemployment? Do many young people want to become entrepreneurs?

3. In your opinion, why do some good businesses fail?

Today's Lesson: How to Start a Successful Business

A   Traditionally, age is respected in Korea. However, you wouldn't know it from watching Chon Ki Son lecture a group of businessmen—many of whom are older than he—as he teaches them successful entrepreneurship, how to succeed in business. "There are three things you should never do," Chon warns. "Never go bankrupt. Don't buy unnecessary real estate. And remember not to expand too fast." 5 Chon's audience writes down everything he says. In a country that for decades favored huge corporations over small, innovative firms—and has suffered from the choice—Chon is lecturing on economic survival in a new era.

B   The course is run by the Korean Advanced Institute for Science and Technology (KAIST), one of the country's elite colleges. Named the High Tech Venture 10 Center, it is located at the KAIST campus in the city of Teajon, 150 km south of Seoul. It's so popular that KAIST has added an eight-week advanced course that includes a trip to Silicon Valley in California. All the students have big ideas. All of them know how to create a product. What they don't know is how to market or run a company or turn a profit. 15

C   Teaching them the basic principles of entrepreneurship is no easy task. Traditionally, big business in Korea attracts the nation's best young talent but, at the same time, discourages the individual initiative and ambition that encourages entrepreneurship. Now things are changing. The government has recognized that entrepreneurs can improve an economy that has relied too heavily 20 on giant corporations. Meanwhile, hundreds of salarymen who have lost "jobs-for-life" are looking for new business opportunities. "Younger, more progressive people think differently," says Kim Jong Dok, a professor and the director of the High Tech Venture Center.

D   The center is one of 142 business "incubators" around the country busily 25 creating new entrepreneurs. Chon explains to his students the basics of running a small business. Some examples are:

1. When making your pitch to potential investors, be more than fully prepared.
2. Keep a perfect credit record. 30
3. Emphasize that your product is breakthrough technology and has worldwide export potential.
4. And above all: "Don't give up," says Chon. "I know one guy who was discouraged after getting only a few minutes to pitch some investors. After the meeting he saw one of them get into an elevator, so he begged 35 for more time and after that he got a second chance."

E   Park Soo Wong is typical of the new type of entrepreneur. The 36-year-old engineer enrolled at the High Tech Venture Center after quitting the government's Agency for Defense Development, where he designed jet aircraft and 40 combat helicopters. Park has developed a software program that figures out in minutes the most efficient way for automated cutting machines to cut shapes from metal, textiles, or leather. He is convinced that he has a winning product. It's faster and cheaper than current methods, claims Park: "Ten percent of sheet metal can be saved using my program" and it's so easy to use that "my seven-year-old son can do it."

F   Park resisted pressure to take a job with a large corporation and rejected the security and prestige that comes with such employment. He spent two years trying to convince his wife and family that he had real entrepreneurial talent. Finally, he entered his business plan in a competition and won. "Until then, my wife thought I was a typical tech guy with thick glasses and bad hair," says Park. "Now she understands." Park hopes to take his product to market next month. Brimming with confidence, he believes the lessons he learned at school will be the key to his success. "I read 100 books, but it was all dead information," he says. "At Teajon it was all living information."

▲ Park Soo Wong left his job designing airplanes to start his own company.

G   Park dreams of one day listing on New York's NASDAQ stock exchange. But even to get to that stage he'll need more money. That might be a problem. In Korea, it's hard to find venture capitalists. "Most are looking for a sure bet," he says. Traditionally, banks lend money almost exclusively to the giant corporations, rarely to small start-ups. Most start-ups relied on money from "angel" investors like close friends. "In Korea, you need collateral to get a loan. Entrepreneurs who can't prove they'll repay cannot get money from banks," says Kim, director of the venture center.

H   The government is promoting start-ups in hopes of encouraging new jobs. Seoul is making a pool of money potentially available to anyone with a marketable idea. Slowly, Korea is becoming more welcoming to well-grounded dreamers. "Korea is full of opportunity right now. You have to grab your chance," says Chon as he ends his lecture at the High Tech Venture Center in respectful silence.

—Adapted from an article by John Larkin

5 **Understanding What You Read** Answer these questions, and then share your answers with a classmate.

1. According to the article, is it unusual for a young person to teach older people entrepreneurial skills in Korea? Why?

   _____

   _____

2. In your own words, what are two of Chon Ki Son's "rules" for succeeding in a small business?

   _____

   _____

3. What is true for students at KAIST? Put a *T* next to what is true and *F* next to what is false.

   ___**a.** They have big ideas.

   ___**b.** They know how to create products.

   ___**c.** They know how to market companies.

   ___**d.** They know how to run companies.

   ___**e.** They know how to make profits.

4. According to this article, what is the Korean government learning that contributes to success in business?

   _____

   _____

5. Why do you think KAIST students visit Silicon Valley?

   _____

   _____

6. What did Park invent? Why do you think that it took him two years to start his business?

   _____

   _____

7. In what ways does Park represent "the new breed" of entrepreneurs in Korea?

   _____

   _____

8. How is the Korean government encouraging new businesses?

   _____

   _____

6 **Practicing Speculating** Work in small groups and speculate about the following international businesses. Will they continue to be successful? Why or why not? Collect reasons for business success in your discussion.

Business: Will It Continue to Be Successful?	Yes! Some Reasons Why . . .	No, because . . .
Starbucks		
McDonald's		
Apple Computer		
The Body Shop		
Coca-Cola		

7 **Gathering Information About a Successful Business** Choose a business and find out as much as you can about it. Use the Internet or library to get information. Take notes on the information you gather and present the most important points to your classmates.

Organize your information search by answering these questions:

1. What's the name of the business? What's the product it sells or the service it provides?	**2.** How, when, and where did it start?	**3.** Are there one or more innovative entrepreneurs who led this business to success?
4. How does the business market its product or service?	**5.** How has the business changed since it began?	**6.** Why did you select this business? What additional information do you know?

Part 2 Focusing on Words and Phrases

Discussing Business

1 **Matching Business Terms** The article "Today's Lesson: How to Start a Successful Business" uses many words and expressions common in business. Match the expressions on the left with what they mean on the right. Write the letter on the line.

_____ **1.** go bankrupt	**a.** beginning business
_____ **2.** innovative firm	**b.** try to sell
_____ **3.** buy real estate	**c.** series of strategies to succeed
_*f*_ **4.** a winning product	**d.** new and original business
_____ **5.** start-up	**e.** investor who contributes money to a new business
_____ **6.** market	
_____ **7.** turn a profit	**f.** item or service that people want to buy
_____ **8.** venture capitalist	**g.** advertise
_____ **9.** business plan	**h.** client, customer
_____ **10.** make a pitch	**i.** purchase property
_____ **11.** consumer	**j.** make money
	k. lose money to pay bills

2 **Answering Questions about Business** Practice writing about business by answering these questions. Explain your answers.

1. How does a venture capitalist take a risk?

_____

_____

2. What is the relationship between timing and business success?

_____

_____

3. Is it more important to be reliable and traditional or innovative to maintain business success?

_____

_____

4. How can government regulations affect business success?

_____

_____

5. What can cause business failure?

_____

_____

6. Which is most important in determining success in business: knowledge and experience or luck?

_____

_____

3 **Rewriting a Description of a Successful Business** Rewrite your description of a successful business from the Freewriting activity on page 105, using expressions and vocabulary from this section.

4 **Writing a Paragraph About a Company You Invent** Imagine that you and your classmates are cofounders of a very successful company. In a paragraph, describe the company and explain your business plan.

5 **Comparing Business Success with Other Types of Success** Does success in other areas of life (education, fine arts, sports, etc.) require the same qualities as success in business? Write a one-paragraph response to this question using specific examples.

Part 3 Organizing and Developing Your Ideas

Paragraph Coherence Through Pronouns, Keys Words, and Paraphrasing

Review Points
- A paragraph must develop one main idea.
- The main idea is often in the first sentence of a paragraph.
- The rest of the paragraph explains, illustrates, and expands the main idea.

> **New Points: Coherence**
> - *Coherence* means a "logical or natural connection."
> - A paragraph is easier to read if the sentences in it move smoothly from one to the other. This is called *coherence.*
> - Writers achieve coherence by connecting sentences through linking ideas and the use of pronouns, repetition of key words, and paraphrases.

EXAMPLES OF COHERENCE

- Writers connect sentences by using pronouns to refer to nouns already mentioned.

Example

Park resisted pressure to take a job with a large corporation and rejected the security and prestige that comes with such employment. He spent two years trying to convince his wife and family that he had real entrepreneurial talent. Finally, he entered his business plan in a competition and won.

- Writers repeat key words and ideas to move smoothly from one sentence to another.

Example

Success in business results from a *willingness to take risks*. This *risk tolerance* is one of the most important qualities that leads to business success. Entrepreneurs *willing to take risks* will move ahead in a new business venture with confidence despite the possibility of failure.

- Writers also paraphrase, restating words or expressions from a previous sentence. Paraphrasing reduces repetition but builds coherence by reminding the reader of the important points.

Example

Lamond said private investors in Silicon Valley, unlike those in Europe, are eager to invest in start-ups. He also said that risk-takers are rewarded and looked up to in Silicon Valley, and that people who try to break the mold are not regarded highly in a conservative country like Germany or France.

1 **Recongnizing Key Concepts** In the following paragraphs, the key words and concepts in the topic sentences are circled. Read each paragraph carefully, find the words and expressions that recall the key concepts, and underline them.

A. Public accounting consists largely of auditing and tax services. An audit is a review of an organization's financial records. Auditing is usually performed at fixed intervals of time—perhaps quarterly, semiannually, or annually. And as the tax laws have grown increasingly complex, corporations as well as individuals have had to utilize the services of accountants in preparing their tax forms. Businesses, government agencies, and nonprofit organizations all employ public accountants either regularly or on a part-time basis.

B. The best-run companies establish strong corporate values and also have entrepreneurs who live according to those values. These businesses transmit the essential qualities of their companies to other people. This kind of leadership is called "value-driven style." A good example of this type of leadership is J. Willard Marriott, Sr., founder of the Marriott Corporation, who read every single complaint card that came into that hotel and restaurant company until he was over 80 years old.

2 Recongnizing Key Ideas in Topic Sentences Read the following paragraphs. Find the key ideas in the topic sentences and circle them. Then identify the words and expressions that recall the key concepts by underlining them.

A. Nations use the capital of other nations to build their industrial bases. This capital is used to build factories and develop mines, among other things. For example, the railroads of the United States and South America were built by British capital. This capital paid for the costs of construction, including materials, the wages of the workers, and the locomotives and freight cars. More recently, American, Japanese, and European corporations provided funds to explore for oil and to build new automobile, steel, and chemical plants around the world.

B. Shaklee Corporation was one of the most successful companies in San Francisco because the managers understood the importance of giving both within and outside the corporation. It was successful because top-level management cared about the welfare of their employees as well as the community in which they did business.

▲ Healthier employees make better employees

Their employees had access to free fruit-juice bars and the use of the company's indoor health facility with its 8,000-square-foot track and cardiovascular clinic. Once a year, the headquarters closed for the day so employees could spend it at Golden Gate Park participating in athletic events. Shaklee Corporation gave to the community as well. They sponsored the Adopt-an-Animal program at the San Francisco Zoo. They helped keep the Golden Gate Park Band alive by sponsoring the musicians for one month of the year and enlisting 11 other companies as monthly sponsors.

3 **Completing Topic Sentences and Paragraphs** The following is a topic sentence "starter." First, complete the sentence with your idea, and then write a paragraph supporting it.

To be successful in business, one must make sure that _____

_____

_____

_____

_____

4 **Writing Synonyms for Key Words and Phrases** When you are writing, it helps to think quickly of synonyms of words and phrases to avoid repetition. Practice this by writing synonyms for the words or phrases on the left.

Business Words and Expressions	Synonyms
Make a profit	
Successful entrepreneurship	
Business	
Customers	
Employer	
Innovative	
Research and development	

5 **Rewriting Paragraphs for Coherence** Rewrite the following paragraphs so that they are more coherent. Repeat key words and ideas to remind the reader of the main idea; use pronouns and paraphrases to reduce repetition.

A. In Mexico, one of the most important elements for success in the business world is the relationships you have. You may be a good student and a diligent worker, but you still need relationships. If you don't have good relationships, you may not even be able to find a job. And if you don't have good relationships, once you've found a job, you may not be able to move up in the company. Good relationships influence how much money you make, too. So establishing good relationships is extremely important for people who want to succeed in business in Mexico.

B. The most successful businesses are stubborn and inflexible. Their employers insist on doing things their way. It is their stubbornness and inflexibility that allows them to maintain high standards and not compromise. Stubbornness and inflexibility allow Mrs. Fields to sell only cookies that are soft and warm. Stubbornness and inflexibility push Burger King to flame-broil their burgers. Stubbornness and inflexibility lead to success.

Review Points
- An introduction prepares the reader for the essay.
- One kind of introduction is the general-to-specific; its form is like an upside-down triangle.

Conclusions

New Points: Conclusions
- A conclusion prepares the reader for the end of your essay, giving a feeling of completion.
- A conclusion restates the main idea and important supporting points of the essay.

WRITING CONCLUSIONS

One type of conclusion—a specific-to-general conclusion—begins with a restatement of your thesis and then moves on to two or three increasingly general statements on the topic as a whole.

Study this example of a conclusion:

> So an entrepreneur's resilience helps assure success when starting a new business. Resilience is valuable for more than business: it allows people to learn new skills, recover from unexpected events, and face challenges with optimism. Resilience brings success to all parts of one's life and many types of endeavors. Notice how the sentences in the example move from specific to general, in the reverse

order of the introduction triangle:

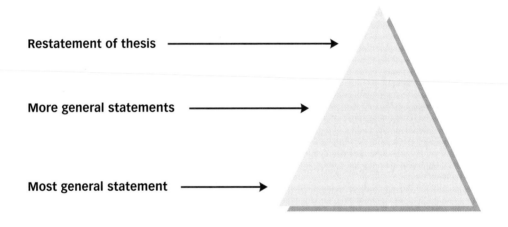

Restatement of thesis ————————————➤

More general statements ———————➤

Most general statement ———————➤

---

6 **Working Together to Complete Conclusions** Following are the first sentences of four different conclusions. Working in small groups, discuss some additional, more specific ideas that each conclusion could contain. Then complete each conclusion, using the ideas you discussed.

1. In conclusion, it's who you know rather than what you know that determines how far you will progress in your political career.

2. Top executives of large corporations agree that listening carefully to potential customers brings success.

3. In conclusion, there is more to life than earning a great deal of money and obtaining a position of power.

4. Therefore, starting a small business is an excellent way for an immigrant to earn a living in his or her new home.

7 **Rewriting Conclusions from a Past Essay** Rewrite the conclusions for at least two of your previous essays, using what you've learned in this chapter.

Writing Product

8 **Writing About Success in Business** Use what you've learned from this chapter to complete this assignment:

> Write an essay on what leads to success in business. Develop your ideas by using information from the research you did in Part 1. Use the new vocabulary and expressions you learned in this chapter, and make sure that your paragraphs are clear and coherent. Also, make sure that you have a good conclusion.

Focus on Testing

Conclusions on Standardized Tests

In this chapter, you learned some helpful techniques for writing conclusions in most of your essays. In a timed-writing test like the TOEFL® iBT, conclusions can present special challenges.

In response to the TOEFL® iBT's integrated task (20 minutes long), most test-takers will probably produce 200 to 250 words. On the independent writing task (30 minutes), test-takers will probably produce 300 to 400 words. Since there is not much time or room for everything that appears in most untimed essays, writers have to make choices. Writing a whole paragraph to conclude is not a very good choice for such a short piece of writing. It would make your response seem unbalanced, with a conclusion that is 20 to 25 percent of the entire response.

The best choice is to write only a very short conclusion (perhaps only one sentence) or to write none at all. This may seem strange to you, since most writing classes make a point of working on good conclusions. However, the rubrics for rating TOEFL® iBT responses do not even mention conclusions. The rubrics assume writers will have too little time to craft a nice conclusion. It is far better to spend your time writing a strong beginning and a solid body in your response. These essay parts will influence the raters much more than a conclusion will.

If you do have time for one concluding sentence, write it. This would be a nice way to end your essay without unbalancing it.

Practice

Look at the following concluding paragraphs. Summarize the main message of each in one sentence of no more than 15 words. A, the, etc. count as words.

a. Overall, the reading's analysis of biohazards is more scientific than the lecture's. We must apply science to this dangerous set of threats to human welfare. Only a scientific approach can direct us in a nonpolitical effort to fight biohazards. If we ignore science and act on personal opinion, the future will be very grim for our children and grandchildren.

b. In summary, my training in calligraphy has taught me precision, patience, and a love of simple letters on a page. It has revealed an artistic side of me that I never knew existed. The training has been so influential that I might even become an art major in college. An art that I thought at first was boring has become one of the strongest influences in my life.

c. The reading's view of space exploration is very optimistic. The writer believes humans will one day colonize Mars and perhaps moons like Europa. The lecture makes this seem unlikely. In the end, the truth is probably somewhere between the reading's viewpoint and the lecture's.

Part 4 | Evaluating Your Writing

Use the following rubric to score your writing. Read the rubric with your class, and then give your writing a score. A classmate and a teacher will also score your writing and explain reasons for their scores. After scoring, you will revise this essay or an essay from a previous chapter.

Rubric for Writing About Success in Business

Score	Writing Characteristics
3 **Excellent**	■ **Content:** Writing presents one or more qualities that lead to success in business and develops these through explanation, example, personal experience, or evidence. ■ **Organization:** Introduction engages reader and leads to main idea (thesis statement); reasons and supporting ideas are organized in paragraphs that have smooth transitions from one to another; there is a conclusion. ■ **Language:** Vocabulary and expressions explain and describe business success; new or abstract terms are defined; sentence types are varied and keep the reader interested. ■ **Grammar:** Subjects and verbs agree; common grammar problems (pronouns, articles, and plurals) are minimal so that meaning is clear. ■ **Spelling and Mechanics:** Most words are spelled correctly and punctuation is correct.

2 **Adequate**	■ **Content:** Writing presents at least one factor that leads to success in business and includes evidence to defend this main idea. ■ **Organization:** Introduction presents topic and includes a main idea; essay has a middle and end; supporting ideas are developed through paragraphs. ■ **Language:** Vocabulary and expressions describe topic; sentences are mostly the same type. ■ **Grammar:** Subjects and verbs mostly agree; common grammar problems (pronouns, articles, and plurals) are distracting. ■ **Spelling and Mechanics:** Writing has some distracting spelling and/or punctuation mistakes.
1 **Developing**	■ **Content:** Writing does not present or clearly develop one or more factors leading to success in business. ■ **Organization:** Main idea may be unclear or missing; supporting ideas and details are unclear or too brief. ■ **Language:** Vocabulary is limited and/or there are too many mistakes to understand and/or follow the ideas; sentences have mistakes. ■ **Grammar:** Writing has many common grammar problems (pronouns, articles, and plurals) that are confusing to the reader. ■ **Spelling and Mechanics:** Writing has many distracting spelling and/or punctuation mistakes.

Self-Assessment Log

In this chapter, you worked through the following activities. How much did they help you become a better writer? Check *A lot, A little,* or *Not at all.*

	A lot	A little	Not at all
I talked about successful businesses.	❑	❑	❑
I freewrote about what leads to success in business.	❑	❑	❑
I read an article about entrepreneurship.	❑	❑	❑
I researched a successful business.	❑	❑	❑
I studied business vocabulary.	❑	❑	❑
I practiced writing coherent paragraphs.	❑	❑	❑
I learned about conclusions.	❑	❑	❑
I evaluated my essay.	❑	❑	❑
(Add something) _____	❑	❑	❑

Remarkable Individuals

In This Chapter

Genre Focus: Analysis

Writing Product

An essay about a leader you admire

Writing Process

- Talk about great leaders.
- Read articles about great leadership and a leader.
- Gather information about individuals others admire.
- Use vocabulary and expressions for writing about leadership.
- Practice essay organization by using graphic organizers.
- Practice developing paragraphs by answering questions.

" Leadership and learning are indispensable to each other. "

—John F. Kennedy
The 35th President of the U.S. (1917–1963)

Connecting to the Topic

1 Which current and past leaders do you admire?

2 What qualities make a great leader?

3 Can someone learn to be a good leader? How?

Getting Started

 1 **Talking About Characteristics of a Great Leader** What makes a person a great leader? Do they have special skills or talent? Talk with a classmate and list three characteristics of a great leader.

_____

▲ Margaret Thatcher, born in 1925, was Britain's first woman prime minister. She was prime minister longer than any other British leader in the 20th century. Thatcher changed the image of her country's Conservative party.

▲ Margaret Mead, 1901–1978, was an American scholar. From her writing and teaching, people became interested in cultural anthropology.

▲ J. Robert Oppenheimer, 1904–1967, was an influential American scientist. He directed the laboratory that built atomic bombs used in World War II.

▲ Pope John Paul XXIII, 1881–1963, was pope of the Roman Catholic Church from 1958 to 1963. Under his leadership, the church made dramatic changes.

▲ Alfred P. Sloan, 1875–1962, developed roller bearings for automobiles. He was president of General Motors Corporation for 14 years and then became chairman of its board of directors.

▲ Jean Monnet, 1888–1975, a French businessman and diplomat, was a leader of the movement for European unity after World War II.

 2 **Recording Information About Some Successful Leaders** Look at the photo of Mahatma Gandhi on page 121 and the photos on these pages. According to Howard Gardner, a scholar on intelligence, these people have been successful leaders. What do you know about them? With a classmate, complete the chart below.

Name of Leader	Are you familiar with this person?	When did s/he live?	Where did s/he live?	What changes did s/he lead?
Mahatma Gandhi				
Margaret Thatcher				
Margaret Mead				
J. Robert Oppenheimer				
Pope John Paul XXIII				
Alfred P. Sloan				
Jean Monnet				

3 **Brainstorming About Great Leaders** List at least five people you consider to be great leaders. When did they live? Where are they from? What have they done? What did they change? Why are they leaders? Share your list with your classmates.

4 Freewriting About a Great Leader and His/Her Accomplishments

Write for 15 minutes about one person you consider to be a great leader. What did this person do or believe to be remarkable?

5 Preparing to Read This chapter features two reading selections. The first is an article written by Howard Gardner, and it describes qualities that make leaders. The second is a student-written essay about Julius Nyerere, a former leader in Tanzania, East Africa. Before reading, answer the following questions.

1. What are some reasons people listen to and follow a leader?

_____

_____

2. The following leaders worked for their country's independence. Can you identify their countries? Add names of other independence leaders you know.

Name	Country	Name	Country
Che Guevara		Kwame Nkrumah	
Vaclav Havel		George Washington	
Chaing Kai-shek		King Hussein	
The Dalai Lama		Mikhail Gorbachev	

3. Think of someone who wanted to be a leader but failed. Why did this person fail?

_____

_____

6 Reading About Leaders Read the articles.

Reading 1: Great Leaders in the World by Howard Gardner

A   For a book called <u>Leading Minds</u>, I studied 21 leaders. Some leaders began as scholars (Margaret Mead, J. Robert Oppenheimer). Some led large organizations (Pope John Paul XXIII, Alfred P. Sloan). Others were leaders of nations (Margaret Thatcher), and still others led beyond national boundaries (Mahatma Gandhi and Jean Monnet). This study showed certain characteristics of effective leaders. Successful leaders must be able to speak well in public, to understand other people well, to have the experience of travelling early in life, and of challenging others in authority in a respectful way.   5

B   My study showed that successful leadership is a relationship between leaders and followers. A leader creates a story or a message that significantly affects the thoughts, behaviors, and feelings of a large group of people. A leader's story must be powerful. The most powerful stories are about identity; they help individuals discover who they are, where they are coming from, or where they are going. A leader must also "embody" his or her story: the leader's own actions and way of life serve as an example of the message.

C   Margaret Thatcher's message was an important part of her successful leadership. Her story gave English people a clear direction. It advised people to be thrifty and efficient and concentrate their energy to rebuild their country to a position of international prominence. If people followed Thatcher's vision, a new, stronger, and more vibrant nation could emerge. Margaret Thatcher was able to convince millions of Britons that she embodied the story she told. They believed that she used her wit and energy to accomplish things in her own life and that she contributed personally to the reinvigoration of Britain through her courage during the Falklands War and after a terrorist bombing at the Conservative Party congress in Brighton.

D   The successful leader begins with a simple story but does not end there. What makes Mahatma Gandhi and Jean Monnet great (and different from other leaders) is that, over time, they were able to convince their followers of a more sophisticated story. Gandhi convinced Indians and citizens of other nations that conflict did not have to be violent. Jean Monnet convinced French people as well as citizens and leaders of other nations that Europe did not have to remain a collection of hostile countries. His message was that there could be power, profit, and peace in dissolving or changing the boundaries. Gandhi and Monnet met many obstacles, but, as Monnet once said, they considered every defeat an opportunity. They had the same vision for 60 years and were flexible in their methods of leadership. They changed the thinking of millions of individuals.

Reading 2: A Great Leader
by Robert Masolele

A   Julius Kambarage Nyerere of Tanzania, East Africa, was the first president of the United Republic of Tanzania and a man I greatly admire. As an individual, he was a family man, loyal to his friends and proud of his country. As a politician, he was a man of principle and intelligence. His early days in a village, his education abroad, and his devotion to his country led him to be an exemplary and inspirational leader.

B   Nyerere came from simple beginnings. He excelled in school from his earliest years and went on to attend university at first at Makerere in Kampala, Uganda and then to Edinburgh University in Scotland. As a university student, Nyerere developed his debating techniques and concentrated on history, politics, and English. Upon concluding his education in the early 1950s, he returned to his country.

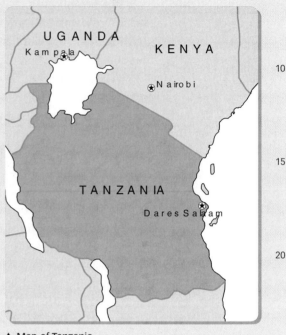

▲ Map of Tanzania

C   In the East African coastal city of Dar-es-Salaam, Nyerere became a teacher but was quite outspoken. He challenged colonialism, which was widespread at the time. Soon he was forced by the colonial authorities to choose between political activities and teaching rather than combining the two. He chose politics. He once said that he was a schoolteacher by choice and a politician by accident. It was at this point in his life that people started to call him Mwalim, a respected title in Kiswahili meaning "Honorable Teacher."

D   As a politician, he started a political party which fought for unity between separate parts of East Africa. His readiness to work with different people was a significant factor in unifying Tanzania and winning independence from England without bloodshed. Tanzania won independence in 1960. After independence, Mwalim and his fellow leaders faced a very tough task in a free poor nation: healing the greatest scar that colonialists had left on Africans—loss of confidence and self determination. Nyerere led his country to self governance and stability.

E   Nyerere worked hard to restore and restructure the young nation and its people by modeling personal integrity and national pride. Nyerere accepted unquestioningly for himself the burdens which he asked other to take up. Nyerere was slow to anger but also slow to forgive humiliation and falsehood. He did not ignore other people's agony.

F   Unlike other world leaders, he retired as president and returned to his village where he expressed gratitude for having been able to work for his people. Though not known as widely as these figures, Nyerere is compared to Mahatma Gandhi, Kwame Nkrumah, Abraham Lincoln, and John F. Kennedy. To people all over Africa, he is a great hero.

7 **Understanding What You Read** First, review the information from Reading 1 and notice how it is organized. Then complete the following chart. The chart shows the organization of Reading 1 by representing general and specific ideas visually. General points are in shaded boxes and less general, or specific, points are listed under them. Study the two examples, and then complete Column 1 of the chart by writing the remaining ideas from the reading.

Gardner's Study of Great Leaders

COLUMN I	COLUMN II	COLUMN III
Types of Leaders	Julius Nyerere	Your Choice of a Leader
Scholars		
Characteristics of Successful Leadership		
Story / Message		

Answer the questions about the readings.

1. What are two characteristics a leader must have?

_____

_____

2. Complete these sentences with information from Gardner's article.

a. Successful leaders must be able to _____ .

b. Stories about identity help people _____ .

c. Great leaders consider defeats _____ .

3. Write five facts you learned about Julius Nyerere in Reading 2.

- _____   - _____

- _____   - _____

- _____

4. Complete Column II of the Gardner's Study of Great Leaders.

5. Does Julius Nyerere match Gardner's definition of a successful leader? Write your answer here and give at least one example. Share your answer and example(s) with your classmates when you are done.

_____

_____

Strategy

Thinking Critically: *Distinguishing Between General and Specific Information*

In the first reading, you read both general and specific information about great leaders. Understanding the difference between general and specific information is an important critical thinking skill. It is also helpful in learning to write well-developed paragraphs. Writers use specific information and examples to support general ideas.

8 Practicing Distinguishing Between General and Specific

Information Look at the sentences below and on the next page and do the following:

- Insert > between the sentences if the sentence on the left is more general than the sentence on the right.
- Insert < between the sentences if the sentence on the left is more specific than the sentence on the right.
- Insert = between the sentences if they are equally general or specific.

The first one is done as an example.

A leader's story must be powerful.	>	Margaret Thatcher's message was an important part of her successful leadership.
Powerful stories help people discover where they are coming from.	_____	Powerful stories help people discover where they are going.
Jean Monnet convinced French people as well as citizens and leaders of other nations that Europe did not have to remain a collection of hostile countries.	_____	Jean Monnet's message was that there could be power, profit, and peace in dissolving or changing the boundaries.

Gandhi convinced Indians and citizens of other nations that conflict did not have to be violent.	_____	Gandhi and Monnet were able to convince their followers of a more sophisticated story.
One characteristic of effective leadership is an ability to speak well in public.	_____	Effective leaders share several characteristics.
A leader must "embody" his or her story.	_____	The leader's own actions and way of life serve as an example of the message.

 9 **Gathering Information About More Great Leaders** Ask at least two people outside class to talk about a person they consider to be a great leader. Take notes in the chart. Share your results with the class.

Name of leader and basic information about him or her	What was the leader's message or story?	How was the person's life an example of his or her message?	What was the result of this person's leadership?

Writing About Effective Leaders and Leadership

1 **Matching Vocabulary About Leadership** On the left are some words and expressions from the reading selections in Part 1. Match them to their meanings on the right. Write the letters on the lines.

Words and Expressions	Meanings
_____ **1.** burdens	**a.** exemplify
_____ **2.** a powerful orator	**b.** independent governance
_____ **3.** a vision	**c.** frank
_____ **4.** model	**d.** responsibilities
_____ **5.** self-determination	**e.** restore
_____ **6.** rebuild	**f.** bring together
_____ **7.** outspoken	**g.** an effective presenter
_____ **8.** unify	**h.** a dream for the future

2 **Expanding Your Vocabulary by Using Word Forms** Make the most of words you know by using related forms. Complete the chart with additional word forms useful for describing remarkable individuals.

Noun	Verb	Adjective	Adverb
example	*exemplify*	*exemplary*	X
•	lead	X	X
•			
•		colonial	X
•			
X	simplify		
•	X		politically
•			

3 Completing Sentence Frames Use the following sentence frames from the reading selections to practice writing about effective leaders and leadership. First, look for these expressions in the reading selections to see how they are used. Then complete the sentences and practice the structures with your own information about one or more leaders you admire.

1. _____ significantly affected the thoughts, behaviors, and feelings of _____. (Reading 1, Line 10)

2. _____ 's actions served as an example of his/her message. (Reading 1, Line 14)

3. _____ was able to convince _____ that s/he embodied the story s/he told. (Reading 1, Line 20)

4. _____ convinced _____ that _____. (Reading 1, Line 28)

5. His/her message was that _____. (Reading 1, Line 32)

6. As an individual, she/he was _____ . As a politician, she/he was _____. (Reading 2, Lines 2–3)

7. His/her early days _____ led him/her to _____. (Reading 2, Line 4)

8. She/he was a _____ by choice and a _____ by accident. (Reading 2, Line 27)

9. S/he did not ignore _____. (Reading 2, Line 42)

10. To _____, she/he _____. (Reading 2, Line 46)

4 Writing a Paragraph About a Leader of Your Choice Write a paragraph about a leader you consider great. Use language from this section and ideas from the readings.

Part 3 Organizing and Developing Your Ideas

Organizing Your Essay

Review Points
- Pronouns, key words, and paraphrasing can help you create coherent paragraphs.
- A conclusion restates the most important ideas and ends the essay.

> **New Points: Organizing Ideas**
> - Order paragraphs so that the ideas flow smoothly from one to another and so that the writing is easy for the reader to follow.
> - You can establish this order with the thesis statement: it previews what the reader is going to follow. Use your thesis statement to plan the order of your paragraphs.
> - Use an outline, a list, or another graphic organizer to help you organize your essays.

STUDYING ORGANIZATION IN A READING

Notice how the thesis statement from "A Great Leader" on page 125 previews the order of ideas in the essay:

> His early days in a village, his education abroad, and his devotion to his country led him to be an exemplary and inspirational leader.

The paragraphs of this essay are organized chronologically. The writer has highlighted important features of Nyerere's life for each of these time periods and uses the thesis statement as a "map" to guide the reader.

- Introduction to essay topic and background information: Who Nyerere was, where he came from, and why he's the subject of this essay
- First main idea: Nyerere's early days and education overseas
- Second main idea: The historical context of colonialism and Nyerere's decision to become a politician
- Third main idea: Nyerere's experiences and challenges as a leader
- Fourth main idea: Personal qualities that made Nyerere great
- Conclusion

Academic essays can be anywhere from four paragraphs long to much longer. The length of an essay depends on the topic of the essay, the number of supporting ideas that can be developed in paragraphs, and the purpose of the essay (to persuade, to describe, to show causes or results, to tell a story, etc.).

1 **Predicting Essay Organization** Read the following thesis statements and predict how you think the essays are going to be organized. First, <u>underline</u> the main idea, and then highlight the supporting points.

1. The gestures people use in Korea when greeting family members, insulting others, and showing respect for elders are different from those used in the United Arab Emirates.

2. Learning to write academic English has influenced me in three ways: I can think in a linear way, I can tell the difference between general and specific ideas, and I have increased self-discipline.

3. Both travel and study in a foreign country result in intellectual and emotional growth.

2 Using a Graphic Organizer Show the organization for one of the essays in the previous activity in a graphic organizer of your choice (outline, list, chart, etc.).

 3 Practicing with Different Graphic Organizers The following thesis statements can be developed in several ways. Use a different graphic organizer to develop the ideas for each of them, and then compare your work with a classmate's.

1. It is essential for people in science and technology to know and be able to use English correctly.

2. Intelligence is not only knowledge—it is also common sense.

3. Success is the ability to do what you want and to be satisfied with yourself.

Writing Well-Developed Paragraphs

New Points: Supporting General Ideas with Specific Information
- To make your writing convincing, support general ideas with specific information. To do this, you can:
  - explain your ideas.
  - provide facts.
  - give specific examples.
  - add specific details.
  - use quotes or statistics.
- Try to answer all of the questions a reader may have. By anticipating reader questions, you can develop support for your ideas.

STUDYING PARAGRAPHS FOR SPECIFIC INFORMATION
The following two paragraphs about Eva Perón and Steve Jobs lack specific information. We can call them paragraph "starters." Read the paragraph starters, and then look at the questions in the chart to see how to develop the paragraphs and make them more convincing.

A. Eva Perón, known to most people as Evita, was a powerful political force in Argentina. In 1945 she married Juan Perón, and a year later he became the Argentine president. Evita became a heroine to many.

B. Steve Jobs is the founder of Apple Computer. His story is one of remarkable imagination and leadership.

Eva Peron

Sentences	Questions
1. Eva Perón, known to most people as Evita, was a powerful political force in Argentina.	How did a woman become powerful in Argentine politics? What was her background? What special skills or interests did she have?
2. In 1945 she married Juan Perón, and a year later he became the Argentine president.	What did Evita have to do with her husband's political role?
3. Evita became a heroine to many.	What did she do or believe to become a heroine?

Steve Jobs

Sentences	Questions
1. Steve Jobs is the founder of Apple Computer.	What is this paragraph about? Steve Jobs or the computer industry or Apple?
2. His story is one of remarkable imagination and leadership.	What did Jobs do that shows imagination? What is remarkable about his leadership?

Finally, read how the answers to the questions in the chart create well-developed paragraphs. The following paragraphs have been developed to answer specific questions.

A. Eva Perón, known to most people as Evita, was a powerful political force in Argentina. During her young adult years, she was a well-known radio and film actress. Perhaps this training helped her develop her excellent speaking skills and her persuasive style. In 1945 she married Juan Perón, and a year later he became the Argentine president. She became his political partner. Evita became a heroine to many. She supported women's voting rights, worked for the poor, and fought for improvements in education. She was able to convince her compatriots that women have a place in government.

B. Steve Jobs is the founder of Apple Computer. His story is one of remarkable imagination and leadership. Jobs got started playing video games, and soon after, he was designing video games. Apple became synonymous for a user-friendly personal computer. As the company expanded and gained success, Jobs concentrated on marketing. Under his direction as chairman, Apple became a billion-dollar company. His original and popular ideas have significantly impacted the technological revolution all over the world.

4 Developing Paragraphs from Questions The following paragraphs are not well developed. Each sentence is followed by questions. Choose at least one paragraph to rewrite and develop by providing answers to these questions or questions you may have. Work with a partner. You may want to do some research to answer some of the questions. You can change words and/or phrases in the original version to make your paragraph better.

▲ Rigoberta Menchu

A. Rigoberta Menchu is a Guatemalan Indian who became a spokesperson for native peoples. (When was she born? Where does she live? Which people does she speak for?) Menchu won the Nobel Peace Prize. (When? Why?) After members of her family were killed, Menchu went into hiding. (When? Where? Why were her family members killed? Who killed them?) Her book has become popular all over the world. (What is the title? When was it published? What is the book about?)

B. Nelson Mandela became the first black president of South Africa. (When? How old was he?) Mandela represented political dreams of black people. (What events led to this? What was Mandela's education?) He was sentenced to life imprisonment in 1964. (Why? When and why was he released? How soon after his release did he become president?) He and F. W. de Klerk shared the Nobel Peace Prize. (When? Why de Klerk, too?)

▲ Nelson Mandela

C. Martin Luther King, Jr., devoted his life to helping people who were poor, disadvantaged, and racially oppressed in the United States. (When was he born? Where was he from? What was his education and training? What motivated him to do what he did? Who were his heroes?) King won the Nobel Peace Prize. (When did he receive the Nobel Peace Prize? What important things did he say? What important things did he do?).

▲ Martin Luther King, Jr.

 5 **Developing Paragraphs from Questions after Each Sentence**

Develop the following general paragraphs by asking and answering questions at the end of each sentence. Refer to Part 1 and your own knowledge and experience to add supporting examples and information. Exchange papers with a classmate when you are finished.

A. Mahatma Gandhi was one of the greatest national leaders of the 20th century. His belief in nonviolent confrontation led his own country to independence and influenced political activists all over the world.

B. J. Robert Oppenheimer was one of the most influential American scientists of the 20th century. He led the development of theoretical physics and directed the laboratory that designed and constructed atomic bombs used in World War II.

C. The American anthropologist Margaret Mead made the field of cultural anthropology popular.

TOEFL® IBT

Focus on Testing

Rubrics and Writing Tasks

Each chapter in this book ends with a rubric—a set of directions for matching a number with certain writing characteristics. Better pieces of writing get higher scores. Raters for the Internet-based TOEFL® iBT use similar rubrics.

The writing section of the TOEFL® iBT involves two tasks: an integrated response and an independent one. Each of these responses is scored according to a different rubric. Some writing characteristics are important in both rubrics and others are important mostly in one. The table on the next page shows some of the high-scoring characteristics in the rubrics:

Both Rubrics	Integrated Only	Independent Only
A good response will have: ■ clear organization ■ a focus on one topic ■ precise use of vocabulary and grammar ■ a variety of word choices and grammatical structures ■ clear connections among ideas	A good response will: ■ highlight the important information from the lecture ■ relate this information to important parts of the reading ■ contain all the information asked for by the prompt, not just some of it	A good response will: ■ have strong supporting details —examples, explanations, reasons, etc. ■ "move forward," (the essay does not get struck on one or two repeated points) ■ show development of the topic (new information in the essay builds on information that came earlier) ■ be unified (all details work together to support a main idea) ■ be idiomatic (it smoothly uses up-to-date English)

The integrated rubric emphasizes content from the reading and the lecture, skillfully used in a response to the prompt. The independent rubric emphasizes organization, vocabulary, and other features that make a response sound smooth and natural. The most important features in both types of writing are relevant content and doing what the prompt asks you to do.

An essay that has a lot of the features emphasized in a rubric may be scored as high as 5. The lowest score on the integrated task is 0, and the lowest score on the independent task is 1.

The full rubrics are available online through the website of the Educational Testing Service, which created the TOEFL® iBT (www.ets.org). Since these rubrics are written for the raters, they may contain vocabulary that you don't yet know. Check with your teacher or another experienced English speaker to clear up any hard-to-understand statements in the rubric.

Writing Product

6 **Writing About a Leader You Admire** Use what you've learned from this chapter to complete this assignment:

> Write an essay about someone you consider to be a great leader. Use vocabulary and expressions you've learned. Organize your ideas and develop your paragraphs according to what you have learned and practiced in this chapter.

Part 4 Evaluating Your Writing

Use the following rubric to score your writing. Read the rubric with your class, and then give your writing a score. A classmate and a teacher will score your writing also and explain reasons for their scores. After scoring, you will revise this essay or you can choose another essay to revise after Chapter 9.

Rubric for Writing about A Leader You Admire

Score	Writing Characteristics
3 **Excellent**	■ **Content:** Writing presents a thorough and engaging account of a great leader and develops ideas through explanation, history or background, example(s), personal reactions, or evidence. ■ **Organization:** Introduction engages reader and leads to main idea (thesis statement); reasons and supporting ideas are organized in paragraphs that have smooth transitions from one to another; there is a conclusion. ■ **Language:** Vocabulary and expressions explain and describe the leader and leadership; new or abstract terms are defined; sentence types are varied and keep the reader interested. ■ **Grammar:** Subjects and verbs agree; common grammar problems (pronouns, articles, and plurals) are minimal so that meaning is clear ■ **Spelling and Mechanics:** Most words are spelled correctly, and punctuation is correct.

2 **Adequate**	■ **Content:** Writing presents at least one reason that describes a great leader and includes explanation and examples to support this main idea. ■ **Organization:** Introduction presents the individual; essay has a middle and end; supporting ideas are developed through paragraphs. ■ **Language:** Vocabulary and expressions describe topic; sentences are mostly the same type. ■ **Grammar:** Subjects and verbs mostly agree; common grammar problems (pronouns, articles, and plurals) are distracting. ■ **Spelling and Mechanics:** Writing has some distracting spelling and/or punctuation mistakes.
1 **Developing**	■ **Content:** Writing does not present or clearly develop a description of a great leader. ■ **Organization:** Main idea may be unclear or missing; supporting ideas and details are unclear or too brief. ■ **Language:** Vocabulary is limited and/or there are too many mistakes to understand and/or follow the ideas; sentences have mistakes. ■ **Grammar:** Writing has many common grammar problems (pronouns, articles and plurals), that are confusing to the reader. ■ **Spelling and Mechanics:** Writing has many distracting spelling and/or punctuation mistakes.

Self-Assessment Log

In this chapter, you worked through the following activities. How much did they help you become a better writer? Check *A lot, A little,* or *Not at all.*

	A lot	A little	Not at all
I talked about great leaders from different parts of the world and from different time periods.	❑	❑	❑
I read an article about great leadership.	❑	❑	❑
I read an essay about Julius Nyerere.	❑	❑	❑
I gathered information about individuals others admire.	❑	❑	❑
I reviewed useful vocabulary for writing about leadership.	❑	❑	❑
I evaluated my essay.	❑	❑	❑
(Add something) _____	❑	❑	❑

_____

Creativity

In This Chapter

Genre Focus: Definition

Writing Product

An essay about a creative person or a creative product

Writing Process

- Talk about creative people.
- Read an article about creativity.
- Gather information about a creative individual.
- Learn vocabulary for writing about creative people and the creative process.
- Study listing signals and sentence connectors.
- Organize a comparison paragraph.

❝So you see, imagination needs noodling—long, inefficient, happy idling, dawdling and puttering.❞

—Brenda Ueland
Prolific Minnesota author and columnist (1892–1985)

Connecting to the Topic

1 How are you creative?

2 What is necessary for one to be creative?

3 How can people be creative in a learning or business setting?

Getting Started

1 **Talking About Creative People** We often think of artists and writers when we think of creative people, but inventors, scientists, and businesspeople also use creative skills. Almost any human activity involves creativity. Look at these photos and share what you know about these people.

▲ 1. Isabel Allende, bilingual author

▲ 2. Joan Chen, actress and film director

▲ 3. Wayne Wang, film director

▲ 4. Alice Walker, poet and writer

▲ 5. Luis Valdez, writer and film director

▲ 6. Steve Jobs, computer company innovator

 2 **Brainstorming About Creative Thinkers** The pictures on these pages show people who are known for their creative thinking. What do you think inspires them? Where do you think writers, artists, filmmakers, and businesspeople get their ideas? With two or three classmates, make a list of factors or conditions that contribute to a person's creativity.

_____

_____

_____

_____

_____

3 **Freewriting About Your Creativity** What inspires you to be creative? If appropriate, choose something you listed in the Brainstorming activity above. Write for 15 minutes without stopping about how, why, when, and where you are creative.

4 **Preparing to Read** The following newspaper article describes how an advertising agency invited a choreographer to talk about applying creativity to work. Before you read, answer the following questions.

1. Have you ever seen a ballet dance performance?

2. What is a choreographer?

3. Is creativity in dance the same as creativity in business?

The Creativity Dance: Advertisers Use Ideas from a Choreographer

▲ Mark Morris performing *The Hard Nut,* also by Mark Morris, a humorous takeoff on *The Nutcracker,* a traditional Christmas ballet

A The ability to think creatively often makes good businesspeople great.

B Creative thinking, sometimes called "thinking outside the box," distinguishes the VW Beetle from a four-door sedan, HTML from DOS, and the iMac from a big beige box. Imaginative thinking is particularly valued in the field of advertising, where creative directors are some of the highest-paid executives.

C A prominent San Francisco advertising agency invited choreographer Mark Morris to discuss how he applies creativity to his work and to managing his business, Mark Morris Dance Company, in New York. Morris has choreographed wildly diverse works that range from a French opera about monsters to cowboy songs. Morris's creativity is overflowing. His ideas pour forth in torrents.

D What advice can a dancer give to an advertising agent? you might ask. Many of Morris's insights are just as applicable in a business office as in a theater. Here are some of the thoughts he shared in a roomful of ad executives:

- Take chances. It's worth the risk of failing.
- Stretch your limits. "Combine traditional and nontraditional forms. Break rules."
- Be adaptable. Don't be afraid to try something new and discover that it doesn't work . . . or that it does.
- Choose employees who have many skills. "It's not just a question of being a great dancer. It's a question of can you dance well, can you get along with others, can you solve your problems."
- Recognize that experienced workers are an advantage. "Our youngest dancer is 23, which often in ballet is the autumn of your career. The oldest is 46. Most of my dancers are in their 30s and it shows. They're cranky, they have a few wrinkles, they don't jump as high . . . but they're also much better at what they do."
- Love what you do. "My life and my job are the same thing. That is fabulous!"

5 **Understanding What You Read** Answer the following questions about the reading selection.

1. Why did the advertising agency want the advice of a choreographer?

_____

_____

2. With which of the following statements would Morris disagree?

   a. Hire older employees.

   b. Don't be afraid to make a mistake.

   c. Your life and your work should be separate.

   d. If you find one successful idea, don't look for more.

   e. Business professionals should be sociable, well organized, and independent in addition to being smart in business.

3. Who is someone you consider to be creative? Would Morris agree with you that this person is creative? Why?

_____

_____

> **Strategy**
>
> **Thinking Critically: _Analyzing Metaphors_**
> A _metaphor_ is a word or expression that is used to explain or clarify a point by describing something else that is similar. For example, "overflowing" is a metaphor used to describe Morris's creativity. The metaphor suggests a river or the contents of a container that are greater than its capacity. The metaphor emphasizes Morris's abundant creativity.

6 **Practicing Analyzing Metaphors** Practice analyzing metaphors from the reading.

1. Another metaphor from the article is: "Being 23 in ballet is 'the autumn of your career.'" What is the literal, or dictionary definition, of _the autumn_? What do you think the writer means by applying it to a dancer's career? Work with a classmate to explain what it means and why it is used.

_____

_____

_____

Now read and discuss the following metaphors from the reading selection. For each expression, explain the literal meaning, and then talk about how they are used in the reading.

2. *thinking outside the box*

_____

_____

3. *His ideas pour forth in torrents.*

_____

_____

7 **Gathering Information About a Creative Project** Research something that is the result of creative thinking. It can be a product, a form of entertainment, a service, or a luxury item. Look for information that explains why and how this creative project happened. Organize your information in an outline like the following one. Try to answer as many questions as you can. Present the results of your research to your classmates.

I. Background about the creative project
    A. How was it developed?
    B. When and where did it first appear?
    C. What does it do/look like?
    D. Which individuals inspired/influenced/made this creative project?

II. The creative project's meaning
    A. What does the creative project represent?
    B. How do people react to this creative project?
    C. Does the creative project improve/enhance/inspire/anger/
       motivate others?

III. The future of the creative project
    A. Will there be additional similar creative projects?
    B. What will happen to this creative project?
    C. How will the creative project be remembered in history?

IV. What else do you know about this creative project?

Part 2 | Focusing on Words and Phrases

Writing About Creativity

1 Matching Words and Expressions Match the following words and expressions for writing about creativity on the left to their meanings on the right. Write the letters on the lines.

Words and Expressions	Meanings
_____ **1.** innovative	**a.** varied; not the same
_____ **2.** imaginative thinking	**b.** really appreciated
_____ **3.** unconventional	**c.** perception
_____ **4.** unique	**d.** do something that doesn't have
_____ **5.** diverse	a guaranteed result
_d___ **6.** take risks	**e.** original
_____ **7.** particularly valued	**f.** only one
_____ **8.** genius	**g.** brilliance
_____ **9.** insights	**h.** "thinking outside the box"
	i. unusual

2 Completing Sentence Frames Use these sentence frames from the reading selection to write about creative projects or creative people you know or know about.

1. The ability to think creatively often makes good businesspeople great.

The ability to _____ makes _____ great.

2. Creative thinking distinguishes the VW Beetle from a four-door sedan.

Creative thinking distinguishes _____ from _____.

3. Imaginative thinking is particularly valued in the field of advertising.

Imaginative thinking is particularly valued _____ .

4. Morris's creativity is overflowing.

_____ creativity is _____ .

Strategy

Making Comparisons
When discussing creativity, it is sometimes useful to write about similarities and differences. On the next page are some examples of sentences comparing creative people.

- Both Gertrude Stein and Ernest Hemingway were innovative American authors who expressed their ideas in short, simple sentences.
- Unlike many other writers, the Korean novelist LeHuang Su moved from the city to the country to write about life in an urban area.
- Picasso was similar to other famous artists in that his extraordinary talent was recognized when he was a young boy.

EXPRESSIONS FOR MAKING COMPARISONS

Review this list of expressions for writing about similarities and differences. Note the punctuation.

Similarities	Differences
X is as (adjective) as Y.	X is . . ., but Y is . . .
Both X and Y are . . .	X is (adjective) + *er* than Y.
Neither X nor Y is . . .	X is more (adjective) than Y . . .
X and Y are alike because they share (these characteristics) . . .	X is less (adjective) than Y.
X is similar to (like) Y.	X and Y are different because . . .
Like X, Y is . . .	Unlike/Like X, Y is . . .
	{ Although / Even though } X is . . ., Y is . . . / Where as
	X is . . . . On the other hand, Y is . . .

---

3 **Correcting Mistakes in Sentences** Correct the mistakes in the following sentences. There is one mistake in each sentence.

1. Like Mozart Beethoven had a father who pushed him in his early years.

2. Although Henry Moore and Geoffrey Chaucer were different kinds of artists and lived at different times they were both inspired and influenced by great artists of the past.

3. Neither LeHuang Su or John Steinbeck were interested in writing about life in the big city.

4 **Practicing Expressions of Comparison** Compare creative people from the photos in Part 1 or other creative people of your choice. Use material you gathered from Part 1 or information you learned from your classmates' presentations. Use five different comparison expressions from the list in this section. Then exchange your sentences with a partner.

5 **Rewriting Your Freewriting** Rewrite your freewriting activity from Part 1 on page 143 using some of the words and expressions you learned in this section.

6 **Writing a Paragraph from Gathering Information** Write a paragraph using your research from the Gathering Information activity in Part 1 on page 146. Use some of the words and expressions from this section.

Part 3 Organizing and Developing Your Ideas

Paragraph Coherence

Review Points
- You can make paragraphs coherent by repeating key words and phrases throughout the paragraph.
- You can also achieve coherence by paraphrasing key words and phrases as you develop your ideas in the paragraph.

New Points: Listing Signals
- *Listing signals* are words that give order to ideas and link ideas in one sentence to those in another; they can make a paragraph coherent. Some listing signals are: *first*, *second*, *third*, and *finally*.
- You can use listing signals to describe events that have a chronological order.
- You can also use them to list points that support your topic sentence, even if the points aren't connected chronologically.
- Avoid using too many listing signals. This makes your writing sound choppy and unnatural.

1 **Studying Listing Signals** Review these listing signals. Then underline them in the following paragraphs to see how they are used.

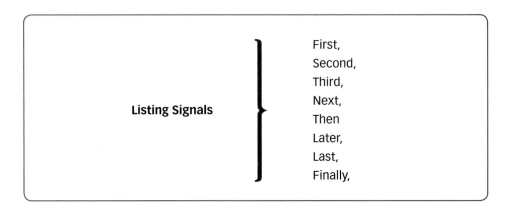

Listing Signals }
First,
Second,
Third,
Next,
Then
Later,
Last,
Finally,

A. I follow the same steps whenever I get ready to write. First, I find my favorite pen and I sharpen all my pencils. Next, I clear my desk and pull out my pad of yellow paper. Then I fix myself a cup of hot tea and set it on my desk. Finally, I turn on the radio to my favorite music station and close the door. Following these steps helps me get ready to write.

B. David's art is different from the work of most artists. First, his pieces are very large and cannot be displayed in small studios. They need big walls and spacious rooms. Second, his art is abstract, combining a variety of techniques: painting, plastering, sanding, scraping, molding, and spraying. Finally, the pieces are very unusual. They present odd forms and original color combinations. David's painting is not conventional.

 2 **Avoiding Too Many Listing Signals** In the following paragraph, the writer has used too many listing signals. With your classmates, rewrite the paragraph by deleting some of the listing signals so that the sentences are more interesting.

Wayne Wang, the Chinese-American film director who became a surprising success story in 1982 with *Chan Is Missing*, always knew that he would succeed in film in America. First, his father named him after the American actor John Wayne. Second, he grew up loving American films and idolizing movie stars. Third, he came to the United States for college. Then he got his master's degree in film. Finally, he was introduced to experimental films that prompted him to break the stereotype of Asians in the movies. Now, Wang is a successful filmmaker whose work—such as the highly acclaimed *Joy Luck Club*—deals with the complexities of being Asian in America.

3 **Writing a Paragraph About Someone's Creative Process** Write a paragraph about the creative process of someone who interests you. You can choose the person who created the project you researched in Part 1 or someone else. Make your paragraph coherent by using listing signals.

4 **Writing an Introduction** In Chapter 5, Part 3, you learned about four types of introductions: general-to-specific, definition/explanation, set the scene, and problem-solution. Take a set-the-scene introduction from one of your past essays and rewrite it using some of the listing signals you studied in this section.

Sentence Connectors

New Points: Using Sentence Connectors
- You can also make paragraphs coherent by using *sentence connectors*.
- Sentence connectors show relationships between ideas in different sentences in a paragraph.
- Sentence connectors link independent clauses and usually come between two sentences. However, if the sentences are short, connectors come after a semicolon (;).
- A few sentence connectors (and listing signals) make writing coherent; too many make your writing repetitive and uninteresting.

Examples:
1. Marcel Proust could write only in bed; similarly, Hemingway had to do his work in a special place.
2. Some people require peace and quiet in order to write. However, others need the stimulation and activity of public places.

SENTENCE CONNECTORS

Study this chart of sentence connectors.

Sentence Connectors		Functions	Examples
Similarly, Likewise, In the same way,	(These expressions indicate similarities.)	introduce a new/additional idea that supports the previous sentence	*Creative writing is a means of communiction; furthermore, it helps people understand their own feelings.*
In addition, Furthermore, Moreover, Besides,			
However, On the other hand, Conversely, In contrast,		show the other side, a contrasting point, or differences	*Filmmaking requires a lot of equipment. However, writing poetry only requires paper and pencil.*
For example, In fact,		expand a point by providing a specific illustration or application	*Carol Evans is a prolific filmmaker. In fact, she produced eight documentaries last year.*
Thus, Therefore, In conclusion,		conclude a point by providing a result; may relate to two or three previous sentences	*People become better writers through the act of writing; therefore, if you want to get published, you should write every day.*

5 **Analyzing Paragraphs with Sentence Connectors** Read the following paragraphs. Write the answer to this question:

- Which paragraph is easier to read? Why? _____

_____

A. Both writing and pottery-making are crafts that require special skills. The apprentice writer and potter are alike because they learn their skills through instruction and practice. The best instruction comes from studying a master, someone skilled in the craft. The potter must begin by observing the master, then working with the clay himself or herself. The writer begins by reading good writing and by identifying the characteristics that make it good. The potter begins with small projects and then, after gaining skill and confidence, takes on larger projects. The writer starts with short paragraphs before attempting essays. Only after a great deal of practice and careful imitation of master craftsmen can a potter form an object of beauty. Only after writing, rewriting, and studying model works can a writer turn out a successful essay.

B. Writers and potters are similar in that they both learn their crafts by imitating masters, people skilled in the craft. They devote a great deal of time and concentration to following these masters. For example, before the potter can produce a delicate vase or a symmetrical pitcher, he or she must spend time watching a master at work. Likewise, a novice writer cannot produce a well-organized essay or even a coherent paragraph without first studying good models. The potter observes the way the expert spins the wheel and forms the clay; then he or she tries to do exactly what the master has done. Similarly, the apprentice writer imitates the work of a master writer. The potter begins with small, simple projects. In the same way, the writer begins with short paragraphs and proceeds to the essay only after mastering the basics. So just as the potter gains inspiration and skill from an experienced artist, a writer learns to communicate effectively after studying the work of master writers.

The smoother paragraph (the second one) has sentence ideas that are linked by sentence connectors. Now go back to Paragraph B and underline the sentence connectors to review how they are used.

6 Practicing with Listing Signals and Sentences Connectors Improve the following paragraph by combining sentences or adding listing signals or sentence connectors. Share your work with your classmates when you are finished.

Steven Spielberg is one of the world's most famous and successful film-makers. When it first appeared, *Jurassic Park* earned more money than any other movie in history. The video of *Jurassic Park* continues to earn even more money. Two of Spielberg's other famous films, *E.T.: The Extra-Terrestrial* and *Jaws*, also set records at the box office. His action-adventure films, *Raiders of the Lost Ark* and *Indiana Jones and the Temple of Doom*, were also block-buster hits. Both of these films starred actor Harrison Ford. The moving drama, *Schindler's List*, was another victory for Spielberg. *Schindler's List* won the Academy Award for Best Picture in 1994. The name Steven Spielberg is well known the world over; his movies are even more famous.

▲ Steven Spielberg directing *Jurassic Park*

7 Rewriting a Paragraph Rewrite a paragraph from a previous assignment in any chapter. Make it more coherent by adding listing signals or sentence connectors or both.

Organizing a Comparison Paragraph

Review Points
- One way to organize a paragraph is to start with a topic sentence, then present examples that support it, and conclude with a restatement of the topic sentence.

New Points: Focusing on Similarities or Differences

- When you write a paragraph that compares people or things, you usually focus on similarities or differences.
- One way to write a topic sentence for a comparison paragraph is to state that X and Y are similar or different and tell how or why they are similar or different.

Example

A writer and a potter are similar in that each learns a craft by imitating an expert.

Here are two ways to organize a comparison paragraph:

1. The first way is to list all the points about X and then all the points about Y. Your paragraph looks like this:

Topic sentence.
XXXXXXXXXXXXXXXXXXXXXXXXXXXXXX
XXXXXXXXXXXXXXXXXXXXXXXXXXXXXX
On the other hand, YYYYYYYYYYYYYYYYYY
YYYYYYYYYYYYYYYYYYYYYYYYYYYYYY
YYYYYYYYYYYYYYYYYYYYYYYYYYYYYY

2. The second way is to describe X and Y for each point of difference or similarity. In this case, the paragraph looks like this:

Topic sentence.
XXXXX YYYYYY XXXXXXX YYYYYY XXXXXXX YYYYYY

---

8 **Recognizing Organization Patterns** Read the following paragraphs. Which pattern of organization does each paragraph follow? Write the example number that matches the style of paragraph on the line.

_____ A. Writing an essay in Japanese is not as difficult as writing an essay in English because the writing rules are not as strict. Unlike an essay in English, a Japanese essay doesn't have to stick to the topic or have a thesis statement. In English, the ideas should be clearly stated and developed. In Japanese, however, it is acceptable to write vague, subtle, and even ambiguous sentences. In an English essay, the conclusion is in the final part of the paragraph or essay. In contrast, the conclusion in a Japanese essay can appear at the beginning or the end of the essay, depending on the style. Whereas a Japanese writer can include two or three main ideas in a paragraph, an English writer must limit the paragraph to one. Because the rules are not as strict, it is easier to write an essay in Japanese than in English.

_____ B. Writing letters is more enjoyable than writing compositions. It is fun to write letters to friends and family since one doesn't have to worry about topic sentences, supporting sentences, or mistakes in grammar. The writer can write about many topics and include as many paragraphs as he or she wants. There is no time limit to writing a letter, so it can be done whenever the writer is in the mood. On the other hand, writing a composition is not as much fun. Each paragraph must begin with a topic sentence and continue with sentences that support it. The writer has to be careful to correct mistakes in grammar and include a paragraph for each supporting idea in the thesis statement. The time for writing a composition is usually restricted, so the writer cannot put it off until he or she feels like doing it. Because of all these rules, writing a composition is much less enjoyable than writing a letter.

 9 **Practicing Organization Patterns** With a partner, choose two creative people or creative projects and compare or contrast them. Both of you should write about the same things (either similarities or differences) but organize your paragraphs differently. When you have finished, exchange paragraphs and discuss which pattern of organization was the best suited to the topic.

Writing Product

10 **Writing About a Creative Person or a Creative Project** Use what you've learned from this chapter to complete this assignment:

> Write an essay about a creative person or a creative project from any field: fine arts, science, business, technology, architecture, engineering, education. Use vocabulary and expressions you learned in this chapter. Try to make your paragraphs coherent. You can develop your ideas by using information from your research in Part 1.

Focus on Testing

Beyond _First, Second,_ and _Third_
In Part 3, you learned about listing signals like _first, second,_ and _third._ These work very well in enumeration tasks— which ask you to list things or ideas. However, only a few tasks on the Internet-based TOEFL®iBT call for enumeration. You must recognize when enumeration is appropriate and when it's not.

Consider the following simplified sample prompts:

a. Do you prefer a very formal class atmosphere or an informal one? Use specific examples and explanations to support your preference.

b. How does the lecture support the reading's claims about controlling poisonous plants?

c. Describe a situation in which you challenged a rule or requirement because you thought it was wrong or unnecessary. Use specific examples and explanations to support your description.

Which of these three is most likely to allow enumeration? It is probably prompt "b," which could be approached by listing several ways:

The first way is . . .

Another way is . . .

A third way is . . .

The other two prompts cannot easily be answered by enumerating things. In fact, an enumeration answer to prompts "a" and "c" would probably seem off-topic to many raters.

Prompt "a" asks for a contrast (between formal and informal classes) and an explanation of reasons. If you only enumerate reasons, you will not fully respond to the prompt. Prompt "c" asks for a description of a past event—not a narrative—and an explanation of your opposition to something. Even prompt "b" can be approached without any enumeration, as an explanation of a support relationship.

This chart shows the best approaches to each prompt and some organizational signals that work in each approach.

Prompt	Approach(es)	Some Organization Signals
a	Contrast	*unlike, in contrast, instead, more* (adjective) *than,* etc.
	Explaining why	*because, since, as a result,* etc.
b	Describing a support relationship	*by* (verb)*ing, both, underlying, as a basis,* etc.
c	Describing a past event	*when, then, while, during,* etc.

Practice For each prompt in the table below, give the best approach(es) for a response and give any organizational signals you know that might help in this approach.

Prompt	Approach(es)	Some Organization Signals
a. Using information from both the reading and the lecture, explain the disagreement over how many planets are in our solar system.		
b. Describe a personal experience in which your attitude toward a friend changed, for the better or the worse.		
c. Explain how information in the lecture casts doubt on the reading's claims about ethanol's fuel value.		

Use the following rubric to score your writing. Read the rubric with your class, and then give your writing a score. A classmate and a teacher will score your writing also and explain reasons for their scores. After scoring, you will revise this essay or an essay from a previous chapter.

Rubric for Writing About a Creative Person or a Creative Project

Score	Writing Characteristics
3 **Excellent**	■ **Content:** Writing presents and describes a creative person or project and develops the topic through explanation of background and origin, purpose and motivation, and results. ■ **Organization:** Introduction engages and informs the reader and leads to the main idea (thesis statement); explanation and description are organized in paragraphs that use listing signals and comparisons to guide the reader; there is a conclusion. ■ **Language:** Vocabulary and expressions explain and describe a creative person or project; sentence types are varied and keep the reader interested. ■ **Grammar:** Subjects and verbs agree; common grammar problems (pronouns, articles, and plurals) are minimal so that meaning is clear. ■ **Spelling and Mechanics:** Most words are spelled correctly and punctuation is correct.

2 Adequate	
	▪ **Content:** Writing presents a creative person or project and includes information that shows how or why this is creative.
	▪ **Organization:** Introduction presents the topic and includes a main idea; essay has a middle and end; supporting ideas are developed through paragraphs.
	▪ **Language:** Vocabulary and expressions describe the topic; sentences are mostly the same type.
	▪ **Grammar:** Subjects and verbs mostly agree; common grammar problems (pronouns, articles, and plurals) are distracting.
	▪ **Spelling and Mechanics:** Writing has some distracting spelling and/or punctuation mistakes.
1 Developing	
	▪ **Content:** Writing does not present or clearly develop a creative person or project.
	▪ **Organization:** Main idea may be unclear or missing; supporting ideas and details are unclear or too brief.
	▪ **Language:** Vocabulary is limited and/or there are too many mistakes to understand and/or follow the ideas; sentences have mistakes.
	▪ **Grammar:** Writing has many common grammar problems (pronouns, articles, and plurals) that are confusing to the reader.
	▪ **Spelling and Mechanics:** Writing has many distracting spelling and/or punctuation mistakes.

Self-Assessment Log

In this chapter, you worked through the following activities. How much did they help you become a better writer? Check *A lot*, *A little*, or *Not at all*.

	A lot	A little	Not at all
I talked about creative people.	❑	❑	❑
I read an article about creativity.	❑	❑	❑
I researched a creative person.	❑	❑	❑
I learned vocabulary for writing about creativity.	❑	❑	❑
I learned how to use listing signals and sentence connectors.	❑	❑	❑
I studied and practiced organizing comparison paragraphs.	❑	❑	❑
I evaluated my essay.	❑	❑	❑
(Add something) _____	❑	❑	❑

_____

Human Behavior

❝ The most important thing in communication is hearing what isn't said. ❞

—Peter F. Drucker
Austrian-born writer, economist and professor (1909–2005)

Connecting to the Topic

1. Do you ever communicate nonverbally?

2. What are some ways to communicate without speaking?

3. What kind of misunderstandings can occur with nonverbal communication?

Getting Started

1 **Talking About Nonverbal Communication** People communicate without always using spoken language. Facial expressions, gestures, clothing, and hairstyles are some ways people communicate without words, or *nonverbally*.

Look at the photographs below. What do you think the people are "saying"?

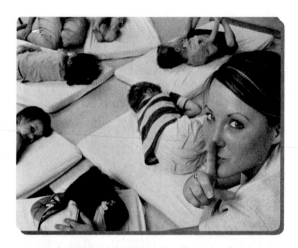

Example: She's saying "hush!" or "be quiet!"

_____

_____

_____

_____

_____

_____

2 **Brainstorming About Nonverbal "Messages"** With a partner, make a list in the following chart of some common ways that one can communicate without words. Share your list with the class.

Nonverbal Behavior "Translated"		
Behavior: What Do You Do?	**Context: Culture & Time Where? When?**	**Interpretation What Does It Mean?**
Hold fingertips and thumb together, rocking closed hand up and down.	Egypt: when someone drives, talks too fast	Slow down!

Sometimes, the same nonverbal behavior has different meanings in different cultures. If people are not aware of these multiple meanings, it could lead to a cross-cultural misunderstanding. The hand gesture in the picture to the right is an example. In Japan, it means "come here," but in the United States, it means "go away."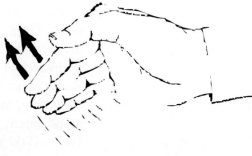

 3 **Sharing Misunderstandings Across Cultures** Do you know of some other nonverbal behaviors that might lead to cross-cultural misunderstandings? Talk with a classmate and write them below.

_____

_____

_____

4 **Freewriting About an Example of Nonverbal Communication** Think of one example of nonverbal communication that you find interesting or unusual. It can be from your culture or another culture. It can be a facial expression, a gesture, a kind of clothing, or a hairstyle. Write for 15 minutes about this behavior. Include details such as how it's done, when it's done, and what it means.

5 **Preparing to Read** The following selection is from an article by Fathi Yousef, an expert in cross-cultural communication. In the selection, Yousef describes an American who misjudged Puerto Rican people because he did not understand the nonverbal communication of that culture.

Before you read, review your list of behaviors that could lead to misunderstandings in Activity 3 on page 165. Which is the most serious? Share it with your classmates.

Nonverbal Behavior: Some Intricate and Diverse Dimensions in Intercultural Communication

A   John Smith has just returned to New York from a vacation in Puerto Rico. John told his friends that since he understood and spoke Spanish, he had no problems communicating with people over there. John also said that he wasn't surprised that the area was not well developed economically. "After all, people there are not organized. Even their business behavior is quite disorganized," John said. "For instance, I once walked to a counter in one of the largest department stores in San Juan, the capital, around noon. The salesman was talking to a couple of native customers; however, as soon as I arrived, he greeted me and asked what he could do for me. I thanked him and told him to help the people he was already serving. The salesman smiled and continued the transaction with his customers. In the meantime, other people arrived, interrupted, were served, and left while I stood quietly furious and waiting for my turn. The salesman never noticed. I tell you these people don't have any sense of order or business."

B   In this example, there is a communication breakdown due to a misunderstanding and unawareness of the cultural nonverbal cues. Although John Smith can speak Spanish when he visits Puerto Rico, he cannot "speak" the nonverbal language of Puerto Rico. He is introduced to a different concept of time. Assuming that everyone follows his own cultural behavior patterns, he concludes that Puerto Ricans have no sense of order or business. John Smith misunderstood the Puerto Rican culture's perception of time. Smith expected a monochronic pattern of communication, where customers are served one at a time and each customer is served in the order of arrival.

Instead, John Smith met a polychronic concept of time, where the salesman tried to serve all customers at the same time. John Smith acted and reacted according to his North American cultural expectations: Time is structured in monochronic segments. Tasks are completed one at a time. According to this system, if customers are not served in the order of their arrival, there should be an apology or an explanation. On the other hand, from the salesman's cultural perspective, he felt he had done his duty and was quite polite. He greeted John Smith as soon as he walked in, then continued with the other customers. John Smith never mentioned what he wanted while many other customers arrived, were served, and left.

c   The salesman's behavior reflects a polychronic concept of time where communication at several different levels happens at the same time. The same behavior can be observed anywhere we see monochronic and polychronic concepts of time meet. Neither person's business or social behavior is inefficient or intended to frustrate or irritate. It is simply a different cultural structuring and meaning of time in communication.

▲ Waiting in line at an ATM in Canada

6 **Understanding What You Read** Answer these questions in small groups.

1. Write what happened in the San Juan department store. List the actions that took place in the order they happened.

a. _____

b. _____

c. _____

d. _____

e. _____

f. _____

2. Pretend you are the salesman in the department store. Tell what happened from your point of view.

_____

_____

_____

_____

3. The following "heads" represent a person's thoughts and feelings. Fill in the heads with pictures, words, phrases, or sentences that represent the thoughts and/or feelings of John Smith and the Puerto Rican salesman.

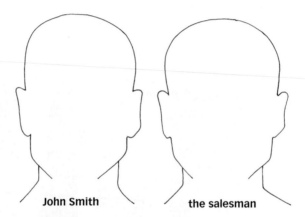

John Smith   the salesman

4. In his article, Fathi Yousef uses several technical terms for describing nonverbal behavior. First, look back at the selection and find the words and expressions in context, and then match the terms to their definitions.

Words or Expressions from the Article	Definitions
_____ **1.** communication breakdown (Line 15)	**a.** several events at the same time
_____ **2.** cultural nonverbal cues (Line 16)	**b.** what our culture has taught us to anticipate
_____ **3.** a monochronic pattern of communication (Line 22)	**c.** signals common in one's culture
_____ **4.** polychronic concept of time (Line 24)	**d.** misunderstanding
_____ **5.** cultural expectations (Line 26)	**e.** one person speaking at a time

Thinking Critically: *Practicing Distinguishing Fact from Opinion*

It is important to distinguish between facts and opinions (or interpretation), especially when trying to communicate with people from different cultures. Facts are objective and opinions are subjective. A fact is an event that happened or something that is true. An opinion is what someone thinks or believes about a fact.

7 **Practicing Critical Thinking** Indicate if the following sentences are facts by writing **F** or if they are opinions by writing **O**.

_____ Puerto Ricans are disorganized.

_____ If you speak the language, you know how to communicate successfully.

_____ Interrupting is always rude.

_____ It is most efficient to serve more than one customer at a time.

_____ It is not necessary for a salesman to greet each customer.

If you wrote **O** for each sentence, you are right. Each of these is a subjective opinion. Now write three facts. Use the example to get started.

Example

Successful communication requires an understanding of nonverbal and verbal language.

1. _____

_____

2. _____

_____

3. _____

_____

 8 **Sharing and Gathering Information About an Example of Nonverbal Behavior** Complete the following activities.

1. Teach your classmates one example of nonverbal behavior from any culture. You can teach a gesture or facial expression or demonstrate how people use time or space. Explain its meaning.

2. Choose an example of nonverbal behavior and find out what it means in three different cultures. You can interview your classmates or go outside your classroom and talk to people in your school, workplace, or community. Take notes and organize your information in the chart on the next page.

Nonverbal Behavior	Meaning: Culture 1	Meaning: Culture 2	Meaning: Culture 3
Person holds fingertips and thumb together, rocking closed hand up and down.	Egypt: slow down!	Italy: serious insult	USA: No meaning

3. Watch at least one half-hour of a television program or a video in which the characters speak English. Turn the sound down. Make a list of as many examples of nonverbal behavior as you can. Write what you think each behavior means. Record your information in the following chart and share it with your classmates. (Soap operas, situation comedies, and dramas are excellent for this activity.)

Title of Program or Film	Date and Time	Nonverbal Behavior	Possible Meaning
The Office	November 2, 9:00pm	Man scratches head and raises eyebrows.	He is confused.

Describing Nonverbal Behavior and Cultural Values

1 **Matching Words and Their Opposites** The following words express cultural values and are useful when writing about nonverbal communication. Match them to *antonyms* (words or expressions that have the *opposite* meaning) in the chart below. Write the letter on the line.

Language Expressing Cultural Values	Antonyms
1. _____ love	**a.** rude
2. _____ to honor	**b.** to admire
3. _____ polite	**c.** dislike
4. _____ disagreement	**d.** be ungrateful
5. _____ show gratitude	**e.** to insult
6. _____ to disrespect	**f.** agreement

EXAMPLES OF NONVERBAL BEHAVIOR

The following words and expressions are examples of nonverbal behavior. Review them in small groups and make sure everyone in your group knows what they are.

winking	kissing on the lips	smiling
bowing	kissing on the cheek	standing close together
hugging	embracing	nodding head
making/having eye	shaking hands	shaking head
contact	shrugging shoulders	raising eyebrows
holding hands		standing far apart

2 **Reviewing and Sorting Vocabulary** Do a word sort by listing five behaviors from page 171 according to when they are appropriate and what they mean. Note the example before you begin.

Greeting	Showing Respect	Indicating Lack of Respect	Displaying Love or Affection
Bowing (in Japan)	Bowing (in Japan)		

After sorting the behaviors, take turns explaining what they mean.

INTERPRETING NONVERBAL BEHAVIOR

The following expressions are useful when writing about nonverbal behavior. Study the list, and then practice writing sentences using these expressions with behaviors from the previous activity. Share your sentences with the class.

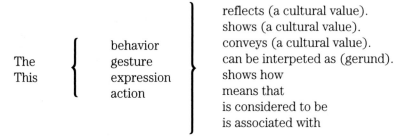

The
This
{ behavior
gesture
expression
action
}
reflects (a cultural value).
shows (a cultural value).
conveys (a cultural value).
can be interpeted as (gerund).
shows how
means that
is considered to be
is associated with

Examples

Carly and Henry hug each time they meet. This action <u>reflects</u> the importance of physical contact in showing affection.

Fumiko bows when she visits her grandmother. The action <u>conveys</u> respect for the elderly.

Said and Maher hold hands when they walk along the beach. This gesture <u>can be interpreted as</u> showing affection.

Tom's teacher gives a "high 5" when the students answer correctly. The behavior <u>is considered to be a</u> sign of approval.

3 **Interpreting Nonverbal Behavior** Do one or both of the following:

    a. Draw a picture or diagram of an example of nonverbal behavior from another culture (not your own).

    b. Find a picture of an example of nonverbal behavior in a magazine, newspaper, or a photograph.

Next to each picture, first describe the behavior and then interpret it (explain what it means). Present your work to the class.

Example

An employee is sitting on another employee's desk in an office. This behavior shows how some workers have very informal relationships at work.

4 **Giving Advice About Nonverbal Behavior** Write some guidelines for a visitor to your culture. What should and shouldn't people do?

Guidelines	Why, or Why Not?
Never make eye contact with your teacher.	This behavior indicates familiarity and in my culture, teachers are highly respected.
1.	
2.	
3.	

5 **Describing Nonverbal Communication** Choose three photos from page 164. Write at least two sentences describing each one. Describe what the people are doing and explain what the behavior means.

Example

Photo 1: A woman is putting her forefinger in front of her mouth. This means "Be quiet."

Part 3 Organizing and Developing Your Ideas

Paragraph Development: General-to-Specific Information

Review Points

- Use listing signals and sentence connectors to make your paragraphs coherent.

New Points: Organizing General-to-Specific Information

- In a well-developed paragraph, the writer supports general statements with specific examples that are clear, relevant, and interesting.
- There are at least two ways to organize general-to-specific information in a paragraph.

1. You can divide your topic into two or more parts and give specific information about each part. This is a "divided" organizational pattern.
2. You can take one main idea and go into great depth by giving more and more specific information about that one main idea. This is a "top-down" organizational pattern.

- Choose a pattern based on how many general ideas and specific examples you include.

DIVIDED AND TOP-DOWN ORGANIZATION

A "divided" organizational pattern looks like this:

1 Topic sentence (most general: has at least two parts)

  2 First part (more specific)

    3 Fact or illustration related to the first part (very specific)

  2 Second part (same level of specificity as the first part)

    3 Fact or illustration related to the second part (very specific)

A "top-down" organizational pattern looks like this:

1 Topic sentence (most general idea)

  2 More specific information about the topic

    3 More specific information about the previous sentence

      4 More specific information about the previous sentence

        5 More specific information about the previous sentence

          6 More specific information about the previous sentence

1 **Answering Questions About Paragraph Organization** Read the
following paragraph on how city planners use space differently in different cultures.
Notice the way the writer has organized the ideas. When you finish, answer the
questions that follow.

(1) A major system for using space in city planning is called the "radiating
star." (2) The star pattern is one in which lines radiate from a central point. (3)
An example of this is in the city of Paris, at the Arc de Triomphe. (4) This monument has several streets and boulevards leading away from it on all sides, like
the points of a star.

▲ Aerial view of Paris' radiating traffic organization from the Arc de Triomphe

1. What is the subject of the first sentence? _____
Is this sentence more general or more specific than the other sentences?

_____

2. What is the subject of sentence 4? _____
Is it more general or more specific than the other sentences?

_____

3. Now look at sentences 2 and 3. Decide whether each one is more general or
more specific than the sentence that comes before and write your answers
below.

Sentence 2 _____

Sentence 3 _____

4. Which organizational pattern did the paragraph follow?

_____

2 **Answering Questions About Sentence Parts** Read the paragraph on
the top of the next page on the subject of how different cultures use space. When you
finish, answer the questions that follow.

(1) There are two major systems for using space in city planning. (2) One is the "radiating star," where lines (avenues or roads) radiate from a central point. (3) The other is the "grid," in which the lines intersect each other, making a series of connecting squares. (4) There are many examples of the star system in France. (5) One is the Arc de Triomphe, a monument that has several streets and boulevards leading away from it on all sides like the points on a star. (6) The grid system is used throughout the United States. (7) New York City is a good example of this system. (8) Over a hundred numbered streets lie horizontally across the rectangular island of Manhattan, each of which is intersected vertically by a smaller number of avenues.

1. What is the subject of sentence 1? _____
   How many parts does it have? _____
   Are these parts the same or different in terms of their level of generality?

   _____

2. What is the subject of sentence 2? _____

   Is it more general or more specific than sentence 1? _____

3. What is the subject of sentence 6? _____

   Is it more general or more specific than sentence 1? _____

4. Now look at sentences 3, 4, 5, 7, and 8. Consider whether each sentence is more general or more specific than the other sentences that come before and after.

   Sentence 3 _____

   Sentence 4 _____

   Sentence 5 _____

   Sentence 7 _____

   Sentence 8 _____

5. Which organizational pattern did this paragraph follow?

   _____

3 **Organizing Ideas from General to Specific** Following is a list of notes about greetings. In Activities 9 and 10, you will organize this list of notes into an outline. First, determine which ideas are general and which are specific. Follow these steps.

Step 1. Write *1* next to the most general idea.

Step 2. Write *2* next to the two major divisions of the most general idea.

Step 3. Find the specific examples. Write *3a* next to the example that supports *a friend* and *3b* next to that which supports *a stranger*.

_____ greeting a stranger

_____ greetings

_____ greeting a friend of the same sex

_____ greeting a friend

_____ greeting a stranger of the opposite sex

4 **Practicing an Outline** Following are some notes about gestures. Organize the notes into an outline. Follow the steps.

Step 1. Write *1* next to the most general idea.

Step 2. Write *2* next to the two major divisions of the most general idea.

Step 3. Write *3a* next to polite gestures and *3b* next to impolite gestures.

_____ polite gesture to get attention

_____ snapping one's fingers

_____ impolite gestures to get someone's attention

_____ waving one's hand

_____ making eye contact

_____ gestures to get someone's attention in the United States

5 **Practicing Organizing Ideas** A third set of notes is about one aspect of nonverbal behavior in Japan. Read and arrange them in the order of general to specific by numbering the phrases from 1 (most general) to 6 (most specific).

_____ nonverbal communication in Japan

_____ the way I bow when I greet my professor

_____ greetings

_____ nonverbal communication

_____ bowing

_____ relative depth of bows

6 **Expanding Notes to a Paragraph** Choose a set of notes or an outline from the any of the activities you've done. Write a paragraph by expanding the notes into sentences. Focus on organizing them from general to specific.

7 **Adding Missing Information to Paragraphs** Now that you have practiced developing paragraphs by supporting general statements with specific information, take a look at the following groups of sentences. Try to figure out what is missing. Supply the missing information, and then write a paragraph.

1. Both travel and study in a foreign country have important advantages. One is intellectual growth. The other is emotional growth.

2. Many people pursue hobbies in their leisure time. One popular hobby is collecting things. Some people collect useful art objects.

Outlines

New Points: Preparing an Outline

You were introduced to outlines in Chapter 7, Part 1. Preparing an outline can make essay writing easier.

- An outline can be as simple as a list of your thesis statement and the topic sentences of each of the paragraphs you are planning to write.
- You can also make an outline more detailed, so that it includes all your supporting information (your ideas and examples) in short, note-like form.

8 **Practicing Outlines (Part 1)** You practiced two kinds of outlines in the previous section. Generally, writers use outlines to plan their writing. Test your understanding of outlines by reading the student essay on pages 179-180 and then completing the outline below.

Shau

Paragraph 1: _____

_____

Paragraph 2: 1_____

_____

2 _____

3 _____

4 _____

5 _____

6 _____

7 _____

8 _____

Paragraph 3: _____

_____

Paragraph 4: _____

_____

Paragraph 5: _____

_____

Shau

▲ Asian-American mother and daughter

A   Do you know that traditional Chinese rarely, if ever, say "I love you" to their parents? In fact, they never say anything to their parents that is similar to the words "I love you." Why do you suppose this is true? It's because a more acceptable way of expressing love for parents is by action. This is different from other kinds of love, so there is a special word for it. This word in Chinese is *shau*, 5 which means "love for parents expressed in action."

B   The word *shau* is easier to understand when we analyze the written character. The character *shau* is made up of two symbols. The first, which symbolizes a son or offspring, is below the second symbol, which represents a person being carried. Together, the two symbols represent a son carrying his father. The 10 inventor of this word was probably inspired by the scene of a good son carrying his weak old father who couldn't walk well. The son shows how much he loves his father. He willingly uses his youthful energy and time to serve his father. *Shau* includes all forms of love for parents.

C   An example of shau is shown in a classic Chinese story about a young man 15 named Shen. Shen was very considerate of his parents. During the summers, before his parents took a nap, he would cool his parents' bed with a fan, so that they could sleep comfortably. During the winters, before his parents went to bed, he would lie in their bed long enough to make the bed warm, so that his parents would not suffer from the cold. Shen didn't need to tell his parents that 20 he loved them because his love for them was obvious through his actions.

D   There are many examples of *shau* which is a loving act towards parents from a son or a daughter. *Shau* is not forgetting about your parents' health.

Shau is waking up at two o'clock in the morning to remind your mother to take her medicine. *Shau* is not visiting parents only on weekends when you don't have better things to do. *Shau* is taking time off work to spend time with your parents. *Shau* is not sending your parents away to an old people's apartment, so that they won't ask you to run errands. *Shau* is letting your parents live in your house, so that you can be at their service when they need you.

E   Therefore, *shau* is love for parents expressed by action. This action is out of a willingness to sacrifice oneself for one's parents. *Shau* is a way to love our parents in the same way that they loved us when we were very young. They sacrificed time and money to love us the best way they know how. *Shau* returns this kind of love.

9 **Practicing Outlines (Part 2)** Read the following well-developed paragraphs on the two main purposes of eye contact in the United States. First, draw an outline of its general-to-specific structure. Then using the same structure, write an outline and a paragraph of your own about eye contact in another culture.

There are two purposes of eye contact in the United States: getting someone's attention and showing that you are listening to the speaker. Using eye contact is a way of getting someone's attention in a public place. You can use this to get the attention of a waiter or waitress in a busy restaurant, an usher in the theater, or a server at a store. The technique is to locate the person you want, watch him or her carefully, and as soon as the person turns in your direction, look directly in his or her eyes. The waiter will come over to you. The usher will show you your seat. The server will take your money.

Using eye contact is also important in North America to show a speaker that you are paying attention. The general American rule for conversational eye contact is to look at the speaker's eyes the entire time he or she is speaking—that is, having his or her turn in the conversation. This tells the speaker "I'm listening to you." If you look away even for a few seconds, the speaker may think that you are bored.

Writing Product

10 **Writing About Nonverbal Behavior** Use what you've learned from this chapter to complete this assignment:

> Write an essay on an aspect of nonverbal behavior. Choose one of these departure points. Use new vocabulary and expressions from this chapter. Make sure your paragraphs are well organized. Try writing an outline to organize your essay.
>
> - Describe and interpret one or more examples of nonverbal behavior in a particular culture.
> - Describe a nonverbal behavior associated with a particular social act in more than one culture. Consider these to get you started:
>   - **a.** Greeting a friend of the same gender
>   - **b.** Greeting a friend of the opposite gender
>   - **c.** Showing respect
>   - **d.** Greeting a stranger
>   - **e.** Insulting someone
> - Describe a nonverbal behavior and how it can cause cross-cultural misunderstanding.

▲ Masai tribe members

Focus on Testing

Writing Introductions on Standardized Tests

In Part 3 of Chapter 3, you learned the importance of good paragraph and essay development, beginning with a good introduction. Writing effective, interesting introductions is a necessary part of any response in the writing section of the TOEFL® iBT.

- An introduction to either an independent prompt or an integrated prompt must do many things:
    - interest the raters
    - lead the rater smoothly toward the main idea of your response
    - show that your response is relevant to the task
    - present a strong, clear thesis statement

A strong introduction is the first step toward a high score for any response.

Practice With one or two other students in your class, evaluate each of the following TOEFL® iBT-style introductions. Does it perform all four functions listed above? What are its strongest features? Its weakest ones? Finally, rank each introduction from 1 to 5, with the best introduction getting 5 and the weakest getting 1. Discuss your opinions with another group or with the rest of the class.

1. PROMPT: According to the reading and the lecture, how do socialists differ from Communists?

    _____ INTRODUCTION: Socialists are very different from Communists. Both the reading and the lecture say so. Their differences are very interesting and form a very long list. Socialists have their beliefs and Communists have their own. Some socialist countries are Norway, Switzerland, and Yugoslavia. Some Communist countries are North Korea and Cuba.

2. PROMPT: Describe a situation in which you had to defend a friend against ill treatment by others.

    _____ INTRODUCTION: Whenever my friend Gary walked into class, half the students in the class called him names like *Hairy Gary* or *Gary, the Human Ape*. Afraid to stand up for my friend, I sat silently, feeling sorry for him. I knew that Gary's long hair and unusual face made him look different from most kids, but I was his friend and I recognized his many talents. I was embarrassed by my unwillingness to speak out in his defense. That all changed in math class, the day before Thanksgiving 2003.

3. PROMPT: Explain how the lecture casts doubt on the information in the reading about robotics.

    _____ INTRODUCTION: The reading about robotics makes several claims about the role of robotics in manufacturing. Movable "robot arms" do dangerous work like welding and riveting. Small, wheeled robots take care of tedious work like cleaning a warehouse floor, and tall, giraffe-like robots arrange products logically on shelves. And this is only a preview of more wondrous achievements to come. But does the lecturer take a similar position?

4. PROMPT: Explain how the lecture supports information about landslides in the reading.

_____ INTRODUCTION: Not very well. The lecturer seems more interested in putting forth an argument for cutting down trees on hillsides. Although the reading gives ample scientific evidence for the dangers of doing so, logging companies turn stable, forested hills into erosion zones. These are perfect places for steep stretches of land to slip and fall in heavy rain. There is no doubt that the companies are motivated by greed, not by any concern for nature.

5. PROMPT: Would you rather take classes that have a final examination or classes that assign a major written project instead of any exam?

_____ INTRODUCTION: Both final examinations and written projects are difficult. I prefer finals. My English is not so strong. Written projects are very difficult. Exams with much reading are also hard for me. How can I pass such a class? How can I get straight As? And what will my parents think when they see poor grades on my report card?

▲ A robotic hand typing on a keyboard

Part 4 Evaluating Your Writing

Use the following rubric to score your writing. Read the rubric with your class, and then give your writing a score. A classmate and a teacher will score your writing also and explain reasons for their scores. After scoring, you will revise this essay or an essay from a previous chapter.

Rubric for Writing About Nonverbal Behavior

Score	Writing Characteristics
3 **Excellent**	■ **Content:** Writing presents and describes an aspect of nonverbal behavior clearly and explains and interprets it thoroughly so that the reader has no questions. ■ **Organization:** Introduction engages and informs reader and leads to the main idea (thesis statement); explanation, description, and interpretation are organized in paragraphs that include information presented in a general-to-specific manner; there is a conclusion. ■ **Language:** Vocabulary and expressions describe and explain nonverbal behavior; sentence types are varied and keep the reader interested. ■ **Grammar:** Subjects and verbs agree; common grammar problems (pronouns, articles, and plurals) are minimal so that meaning is clear. ■ **Spelling and Mechanics:** Most words are spelled correctly and punctuation is correct.
2 **Adequate**	■ **Content:** Writing presents an aspect of nonverbal behavior and describes when and why it is used. ■ **Organization:** Introduction presents nonverbal behavior and includes a main idea; essay has a middle and end; supporting ideas are developed through paragraphs. ■ **Language:** Vocabulary and expressions describe the topic; sentences are mostly the same type. ■ **Grammar:** Subjects and verbs mostly agree; common grammar problems (pronouns, articles, and plurals) are distracting. ■ **Spelling and Mechanics:** Writing has some distracting spelling and/or punctuation mistakes.

1 **Developing**	■ **Content:** Writing does not present or clearly develop an aspect of nonverbal behavior. ■ **Organization:** Main idea may be unclear or missing; supporting ideas and details are unclear or too brief. ■ **Language:** Vocabulary is limited and/or there are too many mistakes to understand and/or follow the ideas; sentences have mistakes. ■ **Grammar:** Writing has many common grammar problems (pronouns, articles, and plurals) that are confusing to the reader. ■ **Spelling and Mechanics:** Writing has many distracting spelling and/or punctuation mistakes.

Self-Assessment Log

In this chapter, you worked through the following activities. How much did they help you become a better writer? Check *A lot, A little,* or *Not at all.*

	A lot	A little	Not at all
I talked about nonverbal communication.	❑	❑	❑
I read an article about cross-cultural misunderstanding.	❑	❑	❑
I gathered and shared information about nonverbal behavior.	❑	❑	❑
I learned vocabulary for describing and interpreting nonverbal behavior.	❑	❑	❑
I learned about general-to-specific paragraph development.	❑	❑	❑
I practiced outlines.	❑	❑	❑
I evaluated my essay.	❑	❑	❑
(Add something) _____	❑	❑	❑

_____

Crime and Punishment

❝ If people are good only because they fear punishment
and hope for reward, then we are a sorry lot indeed. ❞

—Albert Einstein
German-born, Swiss/American theoretical physicist (1879–1955)

1   Have you ever participated in a demonstration for or against a controversial public issue? What was the issue and how did you demonstrate?

2   What kinds of issues are important enough to you that you would consider participating in a demonstration?

3   Do you have friends or family members who work for the criminal justice system? What do they do and what is your opinion of their role?

Getting Started

1 **Talking About Issues Related to Crime** In this chapter, you will think and talk about some issues related to crime. You will practice stating an opinion and supporting it in writing. First, look at the photos. Then read the statements in the chart on the next page. Do you agree or disagree with them? Circle the number on the scale that matches your opinion.

Talk about reasons for your opinions in small groups.

▲ 1. People protesting the death penalty

▲ 2. Struggling to get an education

▲ 3. San Quentin Prison, California (high security)

▲ 4. How can cities prevent young people from breaking the law?

▲ 5. Disciplining a child

▲ 6. Selling handguns

Statements	Opinion Scale Strongly Agree –> Strongly Disagree				
1. The death penalty discourages crime.	1	2	3	4	5
2. More social, economic, and educational opportunities will reduce crime.	1	2	3	4	5
3. Prison does not cure criminals.	1	2	3	4	5
4. Juveniles should be punished in the same way adults are punished.	1	2	3	4	5
5. There would be less crime if parents were stricter.	1	2	3	4	5
6. Handguns should be banned.	1	2	3	4	5

2 Brainstorming Different Points of View on Controversial Issues

The following opinion statements reflect opinions on issues illustrated in the photos on pages 188–189. Read the statements and write some different opinions from those expressed in the statements. Look at the example to get started.

Opinion Statement	Different Points of View
1. The death penalty prevents crime.	■ *The death penalty doesn't discourage crime.* ■ *No one, not even the government, has the right to kill another person.*
2. Everyone deserves a safe home, a quality education, and a satisfying job.	
3. The government should spend more money on education and less money on rehabilitating criminals.	
4. Young people who commit crimes should receive the same penalties as adults.	
5. Strict parenting prevents young people from becoming criminals.	
6. Civilians should not be allowed to buy or use handguns.	

3 **Freewriting About an Issue Related to Crime** Have you ever witnessed or been involved in a crime? Do you have a strong opinion on an issue related to crime or punishment? Choose one of these questions to answer and write for 15 minutes without stopping.

4 **Preparing to Read** In 2001, some paintings by a convicted murderer were displayed in a local art show.

Some people feel that it is not acceptable to display a criminal's art. Other people support the opportunity to show art work, no matter who the artist is. Before you read about this controversy, answer the following questions in small groups.

1. Have you ever seen, used, or bought creative projects or any products created by people in prison?

2. In your opinion, is it acceptable for criminals to display their creative work in public places?

3. Do you think that activities such as painting, writing, and drawing are appropriate ways for criminals to spend time in prison? Why or why not?

4. What should criminals do in prison? How should they spend their time?

5. What should a good criminal system do? What should it not do?

Inmate's Art on Display

A   Condemned death-row prisoner Charles Whitt may never again travel beyond the gates of San Quentin State Prison, but his artwork has left the prison to be displayed in a public art show. Four of Whitt's drawings are part of a public exhibit. To some people, this is an outrage.

B   "I'm really appalled that they allow a death-row inmate to display his art," 5
said Mike Eggert, a recent visitor at the show. "The poor victims can't display their art very well. Everyone forgets the victims," said Jane Alexander, director and founder of Citizens Against Homicide, a victim's rights group. Whitt, 52, was sentenced to death in 1980 for a murder he committed during a robbery. 10

C   Arts Council director Jeanne Bogardus said she believes in the healing power of art. "All of our brochures say, 'Art changes lives,'" Bogardus said. "I believe that firmly because art changed my life." It's kind of sad that people can't just accept Whitt's art," said Patrick Maloney, former art teacher at San Quentin. "Whitt's art is so interesting and strange. It has a strong personal style." Maloney 15
added that the art world is fascinated with work by untrained artists.

D   The prison discontinued death-row art classes about 18 months ago. During the time he worked with prisoners on death row, Maloney said he was surprised by how many inmates had talent. "Every once in a while you meet somebody who can really draw beautifully and you think 'Oh my 20
gosh. If they just had discovered this ability sooner, they probably would have had other options in their lives.'"

---

5   **Understanding What You Read**   Answer the questions about the reading.

1. What are three things you know about Charles Whitt? _____

_____

_____

_____

2. What are the two opposing opinions about Whitt's art on public display?

Opinion in favor of Whitt's art on public display: _____

_____

_____

Opinion against Whitt's art on public display: _____

_____

_____

3. With a partner, think of at least two reasons that support each opinion. List your reasons in a T-chart like this:

Reasons that Support Prisoners' Art on Display	Reasons Against Prisoners' Art on Display
1.	1.
2.	2.

4. What is your opinion of displaying the creative work of prisoners in public places?

_____

_____

_____

Strategy

Thinking Critically: *Recognizing Provable Statements*
Magazine and newspaper writers often make controversial statements about social issues. In order to think clearly about these issues, it's important to know which statements are provable—that is, facts—and which are unprovable—opinions and rumors. Provable statements can be supported by examples and statistics. They are more powerful in persuasive writing.

 6 **Recognizing Provable Statements** Read the following statements referring to the reading selection. With a partner, indicate whether statements are provable (P) or unprovable (U) by circling the appropriate letter.

P   U   **1.** Public display of a criminal's art is not acceptable.

P   U   **2.** Creating works of art can help people recover from difficult circumstances.

P   U   **3.** Art can increase self-esteem.

P   U   **4.** People on death row should not enjoy privileges of ordinary citizens.

DEBATING

In a debate, two teams argue for opposing sides of an issue. Each team tries to make strong arguments to persuade the audience to agree with their position. They also try to make strong arguments against the other team's position. These counterarguments are called rebuttals in a debate. The pro team argues for an issue; the con team argues against the issue.

Most debates follow this order:

Team	Activity	Time Limit
Pro	Clearly states team's position on the issue.	1 minute
Con	Clearly states team's position on the issue.	1 minute
Pro	Presents first argument for team's position.*	3 minutes
Con	Argues against Pro team's first argument.	3 minutes
Pro	Presents second argument for team's position.*	3 minutes
Con	Argues against Pro team's second argument.	3 minutes
Pro	Presents third argument for team's position.*	3 minutes
Con	Argues against Pro team's third argument.	3 minutes
Pro	Restates position in powerful closing statement.	1 minute
Con	Restates position in powerful closing statement.	1 minute

*Arguments can include facts, statistics, personal experiences, and examples.

7 **Gathering Information Through a Class Debate** You are going to have a class debate, a formal discussion of a controversial issue. This will help you with your writing assignment for this chapter. Complete the steps on the next page to prepare for your debate.

Step 1. As a class, decide on an issue to debate. The issue must have two opposing sides. Work together with your classmates and your teacher to select an issue that interests all students. Here are some ideas:

- Penalties for traffic violations are too severe.
- Laws that prevent crime in the community are insufficient.
- Law enforcement practices in our community give police too much power.
- The legal system favors people who have lots of money.
- A particular case (give specific case) was not handled properly.

Write the debate statement on the board.

The death penalty discourages crime.

Step 2. Divide into pro (you agree with the statement and support the issue) and con (you don't agree with the statement and you don't support the issue) teams.

Step 3. Each team member will choose one of the following roles:

a. Team captain: Leads the group and presents the opening and closing statements.

b. Secretary: Takes notes on what everyone says during the planning stage and during the debate.

c. Three people who present arguments: Each person presents one of the main arguments for that side.

d. Three people who make opposing arguments: Each presents a counterargument to the three main arguments given by the other side.

Step 4. Develop your arguments. With your team members, gather information to support your side of the topic. Do research in the library or on the Internet. Work with your team to develop your opening statement, your main arguments, your rebuttals, and your closing.

Step 5. Have the debate and videotape it if possible. Refer to the time limit recommendations on page 193, but you and your teacher can decide on the actual time for each part of the debate. Take three- to five-minute breaks after each side's arguments so that the people presenting rebuttals can make their arguments stronger.

Step 6. Decide who won the debate by viewing the video or by having the presenters and/or the audience vote for the team that was more convincing.

Part 2 · Focusing on Words and Phrases

Vocabulary for Writing About Crime and Punishment

1 **Matching Vocabulary and Meaning** These words and expressions on the left are useful in writing about crime and punishment. Some of them come from the reading selection. Match them to their meanings in the right column. Write the letter on the line.

Words and Expressions	Meanings
_____ **1.** condemned	**a.** young people
_____ **2.** sentenced	**b.** curative
_____ **3.** appalled	**c.** where prisoners live as they wait to be executed
_____ **4.** inmate	**d.** punishment
_____ **5.** outrage	**e.** shocked
_____ **6.** robbery	**f.** legally guilty
_____ **7.** death row	**g.** punishment given by court
_____ **8.** healing	**h.** surprise and anger
_____ **9.** rehabilitate	**i.** not allowed
_____ **10.** banned	**j.** to help to become better
_____ **11.** juveniles	**k.** prisoner
_____ **12.** penalty	**l.** theft

CITING AUTHORITIES

Citing an authority or referring to an expert to support your point of view can make your argument stronger. In "Inmate's Art on Display" by Richard Halstead, two opinions are presented. Look for references that support your point of view. When you refer to the authority for the first time, use the full name of the person. After that, you only need to use the last name.

Example

Lynne Vantriglia, an artist and the founder of Art Behind Bars, believes that everyone has creativity. Vantriglia feels that people can use their creativity for the pure joy of creating, as well as for art's therapeutic value.

The following list contains verbs you can use to cite an authority.

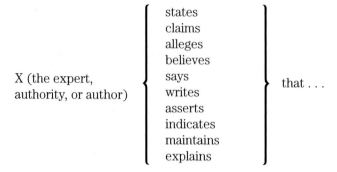

| X (the expert, authority, or author) | states
claims
alleges
believes
says
writes
asserts
indicates
maintains
explains | that . . . |

According to X . . .

One way to cite authorities is to paraphrase their opinions. Study this example:

> Jane Alexander, director and founder of Citizens Against Homicide, feels that murderers should not be able to display their art because it is unfair to victims.

Another way to cite authorities is to use a direct quote. Study this example:

> "All of our brochures say, 'Art changes lives,'" Bogardus said. "I believe that firmly because art changed my life."

You can make your writing more interesting by using both methods of citing authorities.

 2 Citing Authorities in Sentences With a partner, write three sentences related to "Prisoner's Art on Display" using structures and vocabulary from the list above.

_____

_____

_____

3 Paraphrasing Ideas from Previous Chapters Answer the following questions by paraphrasing the ideas from previous chapters' reading selections. Cite the sources.

a. What does Teresa say about San Francisco? (Chapter 1, page 6)

b. What kind of health problems do many angry, cynical people have? (Chapter 4, page 67)

c. What are some ways to build a successful business? (Chapter 6, page 106)

d. What characteristics do successful leaders share? (Chapter 7, page 124)

e. What can lead to a breakdown in cross-cultural communication? (Chapter 9, page 166)

EXPOSING WEAKNESSES IN OPPOSING ARGUMENTS

When you write a persuasive essay, you want to present convincing arguments that support your side of the issue. However, you also need to recognize arguments on the other side of the issue—that is, arguments that are opposed to your position. These are called *counterarguments*. An effective strategy for doing this is to expose weaknesses in these opposing arguments—for example, by predicting how the other side's arguments may have negative results. One way to do this is by using conditional sentences. Another way is to use relative clauses. Look at the following examples:

Conditional Sentences

- If prisoners are not educated, they will never lead productive lives in the outside world.
- Young criminals will become lifelong criminals if they are treated as adults by the criminal justice system.
- If a state abolishes the death penalty, it is communicating the message that it is OK to kill.

Note that each of these sentences can be divided into two parts. One part is called the *if/condition* clause and the other part is called the *result* clause.

---

4 **Answering Questions About Conditional Sentences** Answer the following questions about the three examples you just read.

1. Note the position of the if/condition clause. Does it come at the beginning of the sentence or at the end?

2. Note the punctuation of the sentences. What is the rule about the position of the if/condition clause and the use of commas?

3. Reread the if/condition clauses in the sentences again. What information do they all contain?

4. Note the verb tense used in the if/condition clauses. Is it always the same? What tense is it?

EXPOSING WEAKNESSES IN OPPOSING ARGUMENTS

Another way to expose weaknesses in opposing arguments is to use relative clauses, as follows:

Relative Clauses

- Prisoners who are not educated will never lead productive lives in the outside world.
- Young criminals who are treated as adults by the criminal justice system will become lifelong criminals.
- A state that abolishes the death penalty is sending the message that it is O.K. to kill.

---

5 **Completing Sentences with Your Opinions** Use your own opinions to complete the following sentences by providing the missing clause or by rewriting the sentence with a relative clause. Don't forget to add punctuation where necessary.

Example

if prisons rehabilitate rather than punish

If prisons rehabilitate rather than punish, prisoners will become productive, law-abiding citizens.

Prisoners who are rehabilitated rather than punished in prison will become productive, law-abiding citizens.

a. if (country, state) abolishes the death penalty

_____

_____

b. young people will be less likely to commit crimes

_____

_____

c. violent crime will continue to increase

_____

_____

d. if the criminal justice system in (country) isn't reformed

_____

_____

e. vandalism will continue to increase

_____

_____

6 Practicing Sentences Using the Opposite Point of View Write five sentences of your own, but take the opposite point of view from the sentences in the previous activity. Try to vary the sentences as much as possible. Exchange sentences with a partner and check each other's work when you finish.

Example

Prisoners who are punished rather than rehabilitated in prison will become productive, law-abiding citizens.

a. _____

_____

_____

b. _____

_____

_____

c. _____

_____

_____

d. _____

_____

_____

e. _____

_____

_____

7 Writing a Paragraph from the Debate Write a paragraph based on the arguments you developed for the debate in Activity 7 on pages 194-195.

8 Writing a Paragraph from Your Freewriting Write a paragraph about the topic you selected in the Freewriting activity on page 190.

Part 3 Organizing and Developing Your Ideas

Summarizing

Review Points
- Well-developed paragraphs include a general statement supported by specific information.

New Points: Summarizing

- The purpose of a summary is to briefly explain something someone else has written.
- A summary is shorter than the original work but contains all the important ideas of the original.
- Paraphrasing is an important skill when summarizing.

1 **Answering Questions About a Summary** Read this summary of the essay by Richard Halstead from Part 1 on page 191. Then answer the questions.

When artwork by a convicted murderer on San Quentin's death row was featured at a recent public art show, people's reactions were mixed. One show visitor was angry that a death-row inmate could display his art; another pointed out that the victims can't display their art. Others, however, supported the idea of displaying prison art. One, for example, stated her belief that art has the power to heal. Another, an art teacher at San Quentin, saw real talent among inmates, and felt that if those individuals had received support for their talent earlier, their lives may have turned out differently.

1. How long is the original article? How long is the summary?

_____

_____

2. What is the purpose of the first sentence of the summary?

_____

_____

3. Look at the original article in Part 1. a. How many important ideas are there? b. What are they? Now look at the summary. c. Are the same ideas discussed? d. Are any missing?

_____

_____

4. Note the order of the ideas in the original. Is the same order used in the summary?

_____

_____

5. Note the details, facts, and illustrations in the original article. Do many of these details appear in the summary?

_____

_____

6. Whose ideas are expressed in the summary? How do you know? Do any opinions appear in the summary that are not in the original article?

_____

_____

7. Based on your answers to these questions, what are some guidelines for writing a good summary? Write them below.

_____

_____

_____

_____

_____

_____

 2 Identifying the Best Summary Read the following article, "Berkeley Coffee Clash." Then read the three summaries. First, find the best summary. Then explain what's wrong or missing with the others. Work with a partner.

Berkeley Coffee Clash

There was a victory cry in Berkeley, California, yesterday. The cry came from the French Hotel Café, a little coffeehouse famous for its extraordinary capuccinos, lattes, and sidewalk "salon."

The city had banned the café's outdoor tables because the restaurant did not have a permit. The loyal customers—a devoted group of local writers, artists, dot-com entrepreneurs, and Berkeley intellectuals—refused to obey the ban.

On Tuesday, they organized a protest. They brought their own tables and chairs and set them up on the sidewalk in front of the small café. The French Hotel Café has been a popular "hangout" since the 60s. "There's a culture in our café unlike any others around," said a dedicated customer who led the protest. "It's like a café in Europe. America does not understand the genius of the café. Without the café, modern art would not have happened."

Customers love the cheerful workers behind the counter at the French Hotel Café. Camila and Angel Maldanado, two of the employees, know the names of almost all of their customers. They are expert coffee-makers, specializing in foam designs for their popular capuccinos and lattes.

The protesters claim they held the protest to complain about how long it takes to get

▲ French Hotel Café, Berkeley, California

a permit in the city of Berkeley. Officials, however, state they had been asking the café owners to apply for an outdoor seating permit for three years. Finally, six months ago, the city sent the café a citation and ordered the tables off the sidewalk.

The café owners complained that they "never received any notification." City officials said the owners' statement was a "complete misrepresentation" and said they had sent several notices. When the café owners finally submitted the permit application, the city said it could take as long as 16 weeks to get approval. Meanwhile, customers could be arrested for sitting on the sidewalk without a permit.

"It's going to be winter, and it will be raining," complained a daily customer who has been sipping sidewalk coffee at the café since it opened 16 years ago. Many Berkeley residents complain about city bureaucracy. "It takes forever to do anything!" they say.

Yesterday, finally, a city planning official told café owners, workers, and customers that they could resume outdoor seating without fear of arrest while the permit issue is pending.

"We won!" declared the leader of the protest as he enjoyed his specially decorated latte at the regular tables on the busy sidewalk.

Summary 1. In Berkeley, California, the city council banned tables and chairs on the sidewalk in front of the French Hotel Café. The sidewalk was too crowded and people had trouble walking past the café. Customers were very unhappy with the ban and brought their own tables and chairs to protest the city's action. The city said that the café could resume using sidewalk tables and chairs if they made space for pedestrians.

Summary 2. The article "Berkeley Coffee Clash" describes a conflict between the city of Berkeley and a popular coffee shop. The café did not have a current permit for sidewalk tables and chairs, so the city told customers that they could be arrested. Coffee shop patrons organized and held a protest. They complained about the city bureaucracy and the length of time it takes to get a permit. Café owners sent in their permit application. Berkeley city officials responded to the protest by telling café owners and customers that there would be no arrests while the permit issue was being decided.

Summary 3. In the article "Berkeley Coffee Clash," a regular customer urges us to bring our own tables and chairs to the front of the French Hotel Café in Berkeley, California, to protest city bureaucracy. He claims that the city never warned the café owners that they needed a permit. In addition, he complains that it takes too long to get a permit. He persuades us to visit the café and enjoy the intellectual atmosphere.

3 **Practicing Summary Writing** Choose one of the following articles to practice summary writing. As you write, keep in mind the guidelines for summary writing and cite the author when necessary. Each summary should be about one paragraph in length.

1. "Cynicism and Mistrust Tied to Early Death," Chapter 4, page 67

2. "Today's Lesson: How to Start a Successful Business," Chapter 6, page 106

3. "Nonverbal Behavior: Some Intricate and Diverse Dimensions in Intercultural Communication," by Fathi Yousef, Chapter 9, page 166

4. Summarize an article of your choice. The article can be from a textbook, newspaper, or magazine. Make sure you can summarize the main idea of the article in one paragraph.

▲ Satisfied customers help a business grow

Organizing a Summary-and-Reaction Essay

New Points: Summary-and-Reaction Essays
- In a summary-and-reaction essay, you respond to something that someone else has written or said.
- In this kind of essay, you summarize the main points of the speech or article in the first paragraph, concluding with your reaction, which serves as your thesis statement.
- The rest of the essay supports your thesis statement.

A summary-and-reaction essay looks like this:

Paragraph 1: Introduction and summary of article, essay, or issue you are reacting to
       Last sentence: your thesis (that is, your opinion on what the author says)

Paragraph 2: Body: One argument supporting your point of view

Paragraph 3: Body: Another argument supporting your point of view

Paragraph 4: A third argument supporting your point of view or a paragraph exposing weaknesses in the opposite point of view

Paragraph 5: Conclusion

Note that in the introduction, you lead up to your thesis with a summary of the article you are going to react to. Your thesis presents your point of view—either agreement or disagreement with the author or both—and the body paragraphs explain your reasons for thinking the way you do.

Writing Product

4   **Writing About Crime and Punishment** Use what you've learned from this chapter to complete this assignment:

> Write an essay on an issue related to crime and punishment and argue for or against it. You can write a traditional persuasive/argument essay or a summary-and-reaction essay to an article you read. You can include information from the research you did in Part 1.

(TOEFL® IBT)

Focus on Testing

Citing Sources for Writing on Standardized Tests

Part 2 of this chapter (see pages 195-199) shows you how to use verbs for citing authorities. In the integrated writing section of the TOEFL® iBT, you will cite only two "authorities": a reading and a lecture. The subjects of sentences citing these authorities will usually be:

the reading
the passage
the author
the writer

the lecture
the lecturer
the speaker

These subjects call for different verbs. The subjects that refer to persons *(the author, the writer, the lecturer, the speaker)* can use any of the verbs listed on page 196. A person is able to believe, feel, write, etc. When the subject is not a person but a thing *(the reading, the passage, the lecture)*, fewer verbs can be used. Verbs that can be used are given in the following list.

the reading/passage/lecture
{
alleges
asserts
claims
describes
explains
indicates
mentions
outlines
says
shows
states
}
NOUN CLAUSE (with or without *that*)

According to the reading/passage/lecture . . .

Notice that this list includes "speech" verbs, such as *states*, *says*, and *mentions*. Even though a lecture or a reading cannot actually speak, English treats them as if they could. The list does not include verbs of feeling or thought such as *think, feel, know, believe, like, hate*, etc.

Practice Look at Activity 3 on page 196. It refers you to certain readings throughout the earlier chapters of this book. Change Question "a" to: "What does the reading say about Teresa's attitude toward San Francisco?" Then respond to each question in Activity 3 with one or two sentences in which the subject is the reading, the passage, or the lecture, or which contains the phrase *according to the reading passage*.

Part 4 | Evaluating Your Writing

Use the following rubric to score your writing. Read the rubric with your class, and then give your writing a score. A classmate and a teacher will score your writing also and explain reasons for their scores. After scoring, you will revise this essay or an essay from a previous chapter.

Rubric for Writing About Crime and Punishment

Score	Writing Characteristics
3 **Excellent**	■ **Content:** Writing presents an issue related to crime and punishment and convincingly argues for or against an opinion through facts, statistics, examples, and/or personal experiences. ■ **Organization:** Introduction presents issue clearly and leads to statement of point of view (thesis statement); reasons and supporting arguments are organized in paragraphs that are well developed and persuasive; there is a conclusion that summarizes the main idea and supporting arguments. ■ **Language:** Vocabulary and expressions explain and describe the issue; new or abstract terms are defined; sentence types are varied and keep the reader interested. ■ **Grammar:** Subjects and verbs agree; common grammar problems (pronouns, articles, and plurals) are minimal so that meaning is clear. ■ **Spelling and Mechanics:** Most words are spelled correctly and punctuation is correct.
2 **Adequate**	■ **Content:** Writing presents an issue related to crime and punishment and includes explanation and arguments to support the main idea. ■ **Organization:** Introduction presents the writer's point of view; essay has a middle and end; supporting arguments are developed in paragraphs. ■ **Language:** Vocabulary and expressions describe the issue; sentences are mostly the same type. ■ **Grammar:** Subjects and verbs mostly agree; common grammar problems (pronouns, articles, and plurals) are distracting. ■ **Spelling and Mechanics:** Writing has some distracting spelling and/or punctuation mistakes.

1	■ **Content:** Writing does not present or clearly describe an issue related to crime and punishment. ■ **Organization:** Main idea may be unclear or missing; supporting ideas and details are unclear or too brief. ■ **Language:** Vocabulary is limited and/or there are too many mistakes to understand and/or follow the ideas; sentences have mistakes. ■ **Grammar:** Writing has many common grammar problems (pronouns, articles, and plurals) are confusing to the reader. ■ **Spelling and Mechanics:** Writing has many distracting spelling and/or punctuation mistakes.
Developing	

Self-Assessment Log

In this chapter, you worked through the following activities. How much did they help you become a better writer? Check *A lot, A little,* or *Not at all.*

	A lot	A little	Not at all
I talked about issues related to crime and punishment.	❏	❏	❏
I read an article about prisoners and rehabilitation.	❏	❏	❏
I learned to recognize provable statements.	❏	❏	❏
I participated in a class debate.	❏	❏	❏
I learned vocabulary for writing about crime and punishment.	❏	❏	❏
I learned how to cite authorities and expose weakness in opposing arguments.	❏	❏	❏
I practiced summarizing.	❏	❏	❏
I learned how to write a summary-and-reaction essay.	❏	❏	❏
(Add something) _____	❏	❏	❏

Appendix 1

Spelling Rules for Adding Endings

Endings That Begin with Vowels (*-ed, -ing, -er, -est*)

1. For words ending in silent *e*, drop the *e* and add the ending.

   like → lik**ed**   make → mak**ing**   safe → saf**er**   fine → fin**est**

2. For one-syllable words ending in a single vowel and a single consonant, double the final consonant, and add the ending.

   ba**t** → bat**ted** ru**n** → run**ning**   fa**t** → fat**ter**   ho**t** → hot**test**

3. Don't double the final consonant when the word has two final consonants or two vowels before a final consonant.

   pi**ck** → pick**ed**   sin**g** → sing**ing**   clea**n** → clea**ner**   coo**l** → coo**lest**

4. For words of two or more syllables that end in a single vowel and a single consonant, double the final consonant if the stress is on the final syllable.

   ref**er** → refer**red**   beg**in** → begin**ning**   beg**in** → begin**ner**

5. For words of two or more syllables that end in a single vowel and a single consonant, make no change if the stress is not on the final syllable.

   trav**el** → travel**ed**   trav**el** → travel**ing**
   trav**el** → travel**er**   yell**ow** → yellow**est**

6. For words ending in a consonant and *y*, change the *y* to *i* and add the ending unless the ending begins with *i*.

   stu**dy** → stud**ied**   dir**ty** → dirt**ier**   sunny → sunn**iest**
   stu**dy** → stud**ying**   hurry → hurr**ying**

7. For words ending in a vowel and *y*, make no change before adding the ending.

   pl**ay** → play**ed**   st**ay** → stay**ing**   pl**ay** → play**er**   gr**ay** → gray**est**

Endings That Begin with Consonants (*-ly, -ment*)

1. For words ending in a silent *e*, make no change when adding endings that begin with consonants.

   fin**e** → fine**ly**   stat**e** → state**ment**

2. For words ending in a consonant and *y*, change the *y* to *i* before adding the ending.

   hap**py** → happ**ily**   mer**ry** → merr**iment**

Adding a Final *s* to Nouns and Verbs

1. Generally, add the *s* without making changes.

   sit ⟶ sit**s**   dance ⟶ dance**s**   play ⟶ play**s**   book ⟶ book**s**

2. If a word ends in a consonant and *y*, change the *y* to *i* and add *es*.

   mar**ry** ⟶ mar**ries**   stud**y** ⟶ stud**ies**   cher**ry** ⟶ cher**ries**

3. If word ends in *ch*, *s*, *sh*, *x*, or *z*, add *es*.

   chur**ch** ⟶ churches   ca**sh** ⟶ cashes   fi**zz** ⟶ fizz**es**
   bos**s** ⟶ boss**es**   mi**x** ⟶ mixes

4. For words ending in *o*, sometimes add *es* and sometimes add *s*.

   tomat**o** ⟶ tomato**es**   potat**o** ⟶ potato**es**
   pian**o** ⟶ piano**s**   radi**o** ⟶ radio**s**

5. For words ending in *f* or *fe*, generally drop the *f* or *fe* and add *ves*.

   hal**f** ⟶ hal**ves**   kni**fe** ⟶ kni**ves**

   Exceptions: sa**fe** ⟶ safe**s**   roo**f** ⟶ roof**s**

Appendix 2

Capitalization Rules
First Words

1. Capitalize the first word of every sentence.

   They live near my house.   **W**hat is it?

2. Capitalize the first word of a quotation that is a full sentence.

   He said, "**M**y name is Paul."   Jenny asked, "**W**hen is the party?"

Personal Names

1. Capitalize the names of people including initials and titles.

   Mrs. **J**ones   **M**ohandas **G**andhi   **J**ohn **F**. **K**ennedy

2. Capitalize family words if they appear alone or followed by a name.

   Let's go, **D**ad.   Where's **G**randma?   She's at **A**unt **L**ucy's.

3. Don't capitalize family words with a possessive pronoun or article.

   my **u**ncle   her **m**other   our **g**randparents   an **a**unt

4. Capitalize the pronoun *I*.

   I have a book.   She's bigger than **I** am.

5. Capitalize the names of nationalities, races, peoples, and religions.

Japanese **A**rab **A**sian **C**hicano **M**uslim

6. Generally, don't capitalize occupations.

I am a **s**ecretary. She wants to be a **l**awyer.

Place Names

1. Capitalize the names of countries, states, provinces, and cities.

Lebanon **N**ew **Y**ork **Q**uebec **I**stanbul

2. Capitalize the names of oceans, lakes, rivers, islands, and mountains.

the **A**tlantic **O**cean **L**ake **C**omo the **N**ile **R**iver
Maui **M**t. **A**rarat

3. Capitalize the names of geographical areas.

the **S**outh the **M**iddle **E**ast **A**frica **A**ntarctica

4. Don't capitalize directions if they aren't names of geographical areas.

He lives **e**ast of Toronto. We walked **s**outhwest.

5. Capitalize names of schools, parks, buildings, and streets.

the **U**niversity of **G**eorgia **C**entral **P**ark
the **S**ears **B**uilding **O**xford **R**oad

Time Words

1. Capitalize names of days and months.

Monday **F**riday **J**anuary **M**arch

2. Capitalize names of holidays and historical events.

Independence **D**ay **W**orld **W**ar II

3. Don't capitalize names of seasons.

spring **s**ummer **f**all **w**inter

Titles

1. Capitalize the first word and all important words of titles of books, magazines, newspapers, songs, and articles.

***I**nteractions* *The **N**ew **Y**ork **T**imes* "**T**raveling in **E**gypt"

2. Capitalize the first word and all important words in titles of movies, plays, radio programs, and television programs.

*The **M**atrix* *The **T**empest* *News **R**oundup* *The **S**impsons*

3. Don't capitalize articles (*a, an, the*) conjunctions (*but, and, or*) or short prepositions (*of, with, in, on, for*) unless they are the first word of a title.
*The Life **of** Pi* *War **a**nd Peace* *Death **of a** Salesman*

Names of Organizations

1. Capitalize the names of organizations, government groups, and businesses.

   International **S**tudent **A**ssociation   the **S**enate   **G**oogle™

2. Capitalize brand names, but do not capitalize the names of the product.

   IBM™ computer   **T**oyota™ truck   **K**ellogg's™ cereal

Other

1. Capitalize the names of languages.

   Arabic   **S**panish   **T**hai   **J**apanese

2. Don't capitalize school subjects unless they are the names of languages or are followed by a number.

   geometry   **m**usic   **E**nglish   **W**riting 101   **H**istory 211

Appendix 3

Punctuation Rules

Period

1. Use a period after a statement or command.

   We are studying English.   Open your books to Chapter 3.

2. Use a period after most abbreviations.

   Mr.   Ms.   Dr.   Ave.   etc.

3. Use a period after initials.

   H. G. Wells   Dr. H. R. Hammond

Question Mark

1. Use a question mark after (not before) questions.

   Where are you going?   Is he here yet?

2. In a direct quotation, the question mark goes before the quotation marks.

   He asked, "What's your name?"

Exclamation Point

Use an exclamation point after exclamatory sentences or phrases.

Let the students vote!   Be quiet!   Wow!

*In academic writing, exclamation points are very rare.

Comma

1. Use a comma before a conjunction (*and, or, so, but*) that separates two independent clauses.

   She wanted to work, so she decided to study English.
   He wasn't happy in his apartment, but he didn't have the money to move.

2. Don't use a comma before a conjunction that separates two phrases that aren't complete sentences.

   She worked in the library and studied at night.
   Do you want to go to a movie or stay home?

3. Use a comma after an introductory phrase (generally, if it is five or more words long).

   During the long summer vacation, I decided to learn Chinese.
   After a beautiful wedding ceremony, they had a reception in her mother's home.

   If you want to write well, you should practice often.

4. Use a comma to separate interrupting expressions from the rest of a sentence.

   Do you know, by the way, what time dinner is?
   Many of the students, I found out, stayed on campus during the holidays.

5. Use a comma after transition words and phrases.

   In addition, he stole all her jewelry.
   Common transitional words and phrases are:

also	for this reason	in addition	on the other hand
besides	for instance	in fact	similarly
consequently	furthermore	moreover	therefore
for example	however	nevertheless	

6. Use a comma to separate names of people in direct address from the rest of a sentence.

   Jane, have you seen Paul?
   We aren't sure where he is, Ms. Green.

7. Use a comma after *yes* and *no* in answers.

   Yes, he was here a minute ago.
   No, I haven't.

8. Use a comma to separate items in a series.

   We have coffee, tea, and milk.
   He looked in the refrigerator, on the shelves, and in the cupboard.

9. Use a comma to separate an appositive from the rest of a sentence.

   Mrs. Sampson, his English teacher, gave him a bad grade.
   Would you like to try a taco, a delicious Mexican food?

10. If a date or address has two or more parts, use a comma after each part.

   I was born on June 5, 1968.
   The house at 230 Seventh Street, Miami, Florida is for sale.

11. Use a comma to separate contrasting information from the rest of the sentence.

   It wasn't Jamila, but Fatima, who was absent.
   Bring your writing book, not your reading book.

12. Use a comma to separate quotations from the rest of a sentence.

   He asked, "What are we going to do?"
   "I didn't have enough money," she explained.

13. Use a comma to separate two or more adjectives that each modify the noun alone.

   She was an intelligent, beautiful actress. (*intelligent* and *beautiful* actress)
   Eat those delicious green beans. (*delicious* modifies *green beans*)

14. Use a comma to separate nonrestrictive clauses from the rest of a sentence. A nonrestrictive clause gives more information about the noun it describes, but it isn't needed to identify the noun. Clauses after proper names are nonrestrictive and require commas.

   It's a Wonderful Life, which is often on television at Christmas time, is my favorite movie.
   James Stewart, who plays a depressed man thinking of ending his life, received an Academy Award for his performance.

Semicolons

1. A semicolon is often an alternative to a period. Use a semicolon between two sentences that are very closely related.

   I'm sure Dan is at home; he never goes out on school nights.

2. Use a semicolon before transition words and phrases such as *however, therefore, nevertheless, furthermore, for example, as a result, that is*, and *in fact*.

   Malaria is a major health problem around the world; however, some progress is being made in developing low-cost treatments for it.

Quotation Marks

1. Use quotation marks at the beginning and end of exact quotations. Other punctuation marks go before the end quotation marks.

   He said, "I'm going to Montreal."
   "How are you traveling to France?" he asked.

2. Use quotation marks before and after titles of works that appear within larger works: short stories, articles, and songs. Periods and commas go before the final quotation marks.

>My favorite song is "Let it Be."

Apostrophes

1. Use apostrophes in contractions.

| don't | it's* | we've | they're |

*Notice the difference between:

It's hot. (*It's* is a contraction of *it is*.)
The dog is hurt. Its leg is broken. (*Its* is possessive.)

2. Use an apostrophe to make possessive nouns.

Singular: Jerry's   my boss's
Plural: the children's   the Smiths'

Underlining and Italicizing

The tiles of books, magazines, newspapers, plays, television programs, and movies should be italicized. If italicizing is not possible because you are writing by hand, underline instead.

>I am reading *One Hundred Years of Solitude*.
>Did you like the movie *Crash*?

Appendix 4

A List of Noncount Nouns

Food

bread, butter, cheese, chicken*, chocolate, coffee,* cream, fish,* flour, fruit, ice cream,* juice, meat, milk, rice, salt, spaghetti, sugar, tea

Activities and Sports

baseball,* chess, dance,* skating, soccer, tennis

---

* These nouns have both count and noncount uses. They are noncount when they refer to the item in general. They are count when they refer to a particular item.

I love chicken. (the meat)
The farmer raised twenty chickens. (the animals)
Coffee is delicious. (the drink)
Can I have a coffee please? (a cup of coffee)

Natural Phenomena

Weather:	rain, snow, sunshine, thunder, wind
Gases:	air, hydrogen, nitrogen, oxygen
Minerals:	copper, gold, iron, silver, steel
Materials:	dirt, dust, grass, ice, land, oil, sand, water

Emotions and Qualities**

ambition, anger, courage, fear, freedom, happiness, hatred, honesty, justice, loneliness, love, joy, pride

Social Issues**

abortion, crime, democracy, divorce, freedom, hunger, nuclear power, peace, pollution, poverty

Mass Nouns (Composed of Dissimilar items)

change, clothing, fruit, equipment, furniture, information, jewelry, luggage, mail, machinery, makeup, medicine, money, noise, scenery, technology, transportation, vocabulary

Subjects

art, economics, history, humanities, physics

Miscellaneous

advice, business, fun, glass, homework, knowledge, information, insurance, life, nature, news, paint, publicity, reality, research, sleep, time, traffic, trouble, tuition, work

** Most emotions, qualities, and social issue nouns can also function as count nouns: a strong ambition, a deep hatred, a terrible crime, a young democracy

Appendix 5

Subordinating Conjunctions

Subordinating conjunctions can show relationships of time, reason, contrast, and purpose.

1. Time: when, whenever

2. Reason: because, since

3. Contrast: although, even though, though

4. Purpose: so that

Appendix 6

Transitions

Transitions are words or phrases that show the relationship between two ideas. The most common transitions are used to:

1. Give examples: for example, for instance

2. Add emphasis: in fact, of course

3. Add information: in addition, furthermore, moreover, besides

4. Make comparisons: similarly, likewise

5. Show contrast: however, nevertheless, in contrast, on the contrary, on one/on the other hand

6. Give reasons or results: therefore, as a result, as a consequence, for this/that reason

7. Show sequences: now, then, first (second, etc.) earlier, later, meanwhile, finally

Skills Index

Text Credits

Page 17: Adapted excerpt from *Design for a One-Day Host Family Workshop, readings in Intercultural Communication 5*, by Jim Leonard. *Intercultural Communications Network*, Pittsburgh, PA; page 18: Excerpt from *Models for Reentry Transition Seminars and Workshops* by Jerry Wilcot, James O'Driscoll, Nobleza Asuncion-Lande, and Cal Downs. University of Kansas Communications Studies Dept.; page 20: Excerpt from *Beaux Gestes: A Guide to French Body Talk*, by Laurence Wylie. Undergraduate Press, Cambridge, MA, 1977; page 67: "Cynicism and Mistrust Tied to Early Death" by Sandra Blakesee, from *The New York Times*, January 17, 1989; page 84: from "Nanotechnology: The Science of the Small" by Noah Robischon. *Futurists News*, July 2000; page 106: "Today's Lesson: How to Start a Successful Business" by John Larkin, from *Asiaweek*, October 29, 1999, Vol. 25, No. 43, as submitted; page 124: Adapted from "Great Leaders of the World" by Howard Gardner, from *InterActive Teacher*, February/March, 1996; page 144: Adapted from "The Creativity Dance" by Carol Emert. *The San Francisco Chronicle*, August 12, 2000, as submitted; page 166: "Nonverbal Behavior: Some Intricate and Diverse Dimensions in Intercultural Communication" by Fathi Yousef, from *Intercultural Communications*: A Reader, Second Edition; page 191: "Inmate's Public Art Display Defended" by Richard Halstead, from *Marin Independent Journal*, March 25, 2001; page 201: Adapted from "Berkeley Coffee Clash" by Charles Burress, from *The San Francisco Chronicle*, October 7, 2000.

The publisher apologizes for any apparent infringement of copyright and if notified, will be pleased to rectify any errors or omissions at the earliest opportunity.

Photo Credits

Page 3: © Mario Tama/Getty Images; 4 (top left): © Royalty-Free/CORBIS; 4 (top right): © The McGraw-Hill Companies, Inc./John Flournoy, photographer; 4 (bottom): © T. O'Keefe/PhotoLink/Getty Images; 7: © Royalty-Free/CORBIS; 8: © John A. Rizzo/ Getty Images; 11: © Royalty-Free/CORBIS; 27: © Gary Conner/ PhotoEdit; 28 (top left and top right): © image100 Ltd; 28 (bottom left): © BananaStock/JupiterImages; 28 (bottom right): © Getty Images/Digital Vision; 40: © Digital Vision; 45: © Javier Pierini/Brand X Pictures/ Jupiterimages; 46 (top left): © Royalty-Free/CORBIS; 46 (top right): © Scott T. Baxter/Getty Images; 46 (bottom left): © Keith Thomas Productions/ Brand X Pictures/PictureQuest; 46 (bottom right): © Royalty-Free/CORBIS; 48: © Brand X/SW Productions; 52: © Digital Vision/PunchStock; 57: © Royalty-Free/CORBIS; 58: © ER Productions/Brand X Pictures/Jupiterimages; 63: © Royalty-Free/CORBIS; 64: © Andersen Ross/ Getty Images; 64 (top left): © Robert Brenner/PhotoEdit; 64 (top right): © BananaStock/JupiterImages; 64 (bottom left): © Digital Vision; 64 (bottom right): © Royalty-Free/CORBIS; 65: © Mary Kate Denny/ PhotoEdit; 72: © Getty Images; 74: © PhotoLink/Getty Images; 77: © Dynamic Graphics/JupiterImages; 81: © Digital Vision/PunchStock; 82 (top left): © The McGraw-Hill Companies, Inc./John Flournoy, photographer; 82 (top right): © USDA; 82 (bottom left): © Royalty-Free/CORBIS; 82 (bottom right): © Comstock/ PunchStock; 83: © Kenneth Eward/BioGrafix; 84: © Stock Boston; 85: © Erik Viktor/Science Photo LIbrary/ Photo Researchers; 99: © PhotoLink/ Getty Images; 103: © DPA/The Image Works; 104 (top left): © Alan King/Alamy; 104 (top right): © The McGraw-Hill Companies, Inc./Christopher Kerrigan, photographer; 104 (bottom): © Ramin Talaie/CORBIS; 107: © Seokyong Lee/Black Star for Asiaweek; 113: © Jeff Maloney/ Getty Images; 121: © Hulton/Archive Photos/Getty Images; 122 (top left, top right: and bottom right): © Bettmann/CORBIS; 122 (bottom left): © CORBIS; 123 (left): © Bettmann/CORBIS; 123 (right): © Hulton-Deutsch Collection/ CORBIS; 135 (top): © Reuters New Media/CORBIS; 135 (bottom): © CORBIS; 136: © Archive Photos/Getty Images; 141: © The McGraw-Hill Companies, Inc./Andrew Resek, photographer; 142 (top left): © Szenes Jason/CORBIS SYGMA; 142 (top right, bottom left and bottom right): AP/Wide World Photos; 143 (left): The Everett Collection; 143 (right): AP/Wide World Photos; 144: © Robbie Jack/CORBIS; 154: The Everett Collection; 158: © Dynamic Graphics/JupiterImages; 160: © Digital Vision; 163: © Tanya Constantine/Brand X Pictures/Jupiterimages; 164 (top left): © BananaStock/ PunchStock; 164 (top right): © The McGraw-Hill Companies, Inc./Jill Braaten, photographer; 164 (bottom left): © Digital Vision; 164 (bottom right): © Image100 Ltd; 167 (left): © Paul Conklin/PhotoEdit; 167 (right): © Doug Menuez/Getty Images; 173: © Michael Newman/PhotoEdit; 175: © Yann Arthus-Bertrand/CORBIS; 179: © Digital Vision/ PunchStock; 181: © Brand X Pictures/PunchStock; 183: © PhotoDisc/Getty Images; 187: © The McGraw-Hill Companies, Inc./Christopher Kerrigan, photographer; 188 (top left): © George W. Gardmer/Stock Boston; 188 (top right): © Getty Images; 188 (bottom left): © Royalty-Free/CORBIS; 188 (bottom right): © BananaStock/ JupiterImages; 189 (left): © Digital Vision/PunchStock; 189 (right): © Bob Daemmrich/ The Image Works; 202: © John Jung; 203: © Ryan McVay/Getty Images.